ARCHITECTURE AND DESIGN
1970-1990

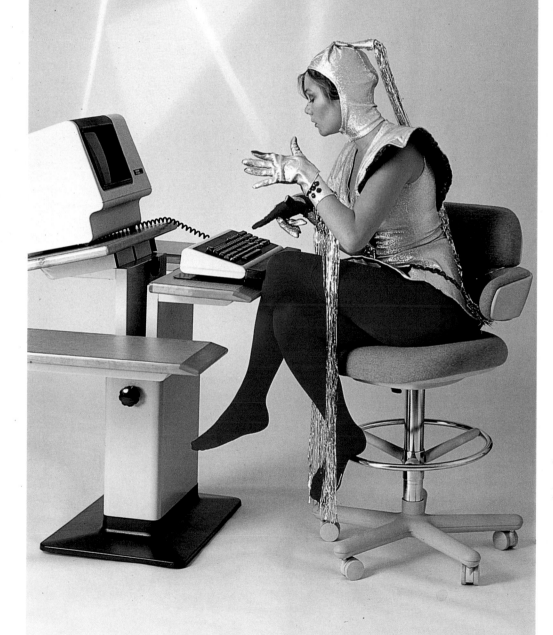

Office workers now ride in tandem with Space-Age technology that brings efficiency and productivity to a job.

NEW IDEAS IN AMERICA

ARCHITECTURE AND DESIGN
1970-1990

KENT BLOOMER
Professor of Architectural Design, and director, Undergraduate Studies, Yale University School of Architecture, New Haven, Connecticut

THOM MAYNE
Principal, Morphosis Architects, Santa Monica, California, and member of the board of directors, Southern California Institute of Architecture.

PAUL HAIGH
Principal, Haigh Space Architecture + Design, New York, New York

ADVISORY BOARD FOR THIS BOOK:

MICHAEL McCOY
Co-Chairman, Interiors and Industrial Design Department, Cranbrook Academy of Art, Bloomfield Hills, Michigan.

RAUL DE ARMAS
Partner in Charge of Interior Design, Skidmore, Owings & Merrill, New York, New York, and former member of the board of advisors, School of Architecture, Cornell University.

ALEXIA LALLI
Coordinator, Aspen Design Conference 1983-88, and communications consultant, Lalli Associates, New York, New York.

Harry N. Abrams, Inc.,

2

NEW IDEAS IN AMERICA

Beverly Russell

DAVID SCOTT SLOVIC
Henry Luce Professor of Architecture and
Society, Tulane University, and principal,
David Slovic Associates, Philadelphia,
Pennsylvania.

MARGARET McCURRY
Principal, Tigerman McCurry, Chicago,
Illinois.

ELIZABETH SVERBEYEFF
Senior architectural editor, *House and Garden*,
New York, New York.

JEFFREY OSBORNE
Formerly design director, Knoll International, and presently design consultant, New York, New York.

STANLEY TIGERMAN
Principal, Tigerman McCurry, Chicago,
Illinois, and director, Department of
Architecture, University of Chicago.

LIGIA RAVÉ
Henry Luce Professor
of Architecture and
Society, Tulane University, and principal,
David Slovic Associates, Philadelphia,
Pennsylvania.

Publishers, New York

Engaging spectators in participatory activities, the Wonder Wall at the New Orleans Expo in 1984 combined the haptic and the syncretic.

Library of Congress Cataloging-in-Publication Data

Russell, Beverly.
    Architecture and design, 1970–1990 : new ideas in America /
Beverly Russell.
        p.   cm.
    Includes index.
    ISBN 0-8109-1890-0
    1. Architecture, Modern—20th century—United States—Themes,
motives. 2. Architecture—United States—Themes, motives.
I. Title.
NA712.R86 1989
720'.973—dc19   89–210

Launched in 1985, the Swid Powell Collection brought the designs of world-class architects to the tabletop. The black and white pattern, "Notebook," by Robert Venturi.

EDITOR: LOIS BROWN

DESIGNER: SAMUEL N. ANTUPIT

Copyright ©1989 Beverly Russell

Published in 1989 by Harry N. Abrams, Incorporated, New York

A Times Mirror Company   Printed and bound in Japan

CONTENTS

Early Post-Modern office for CBS Theatrical Films designed in 1982 with classical motifs by Voorsanger & Mills has architectonic monumentality.

The Brazilito table by Peter Shire expresses the new design code of the late 1980s, which is preoccupied with a search for a reconstruction of Modern design theory through deconstruction of ideas.

Pristine monochromatic
showroom for
Artemide by Vignelli
Associates demonstrates
the crisp, reductive
geometry of pure
Modernism.

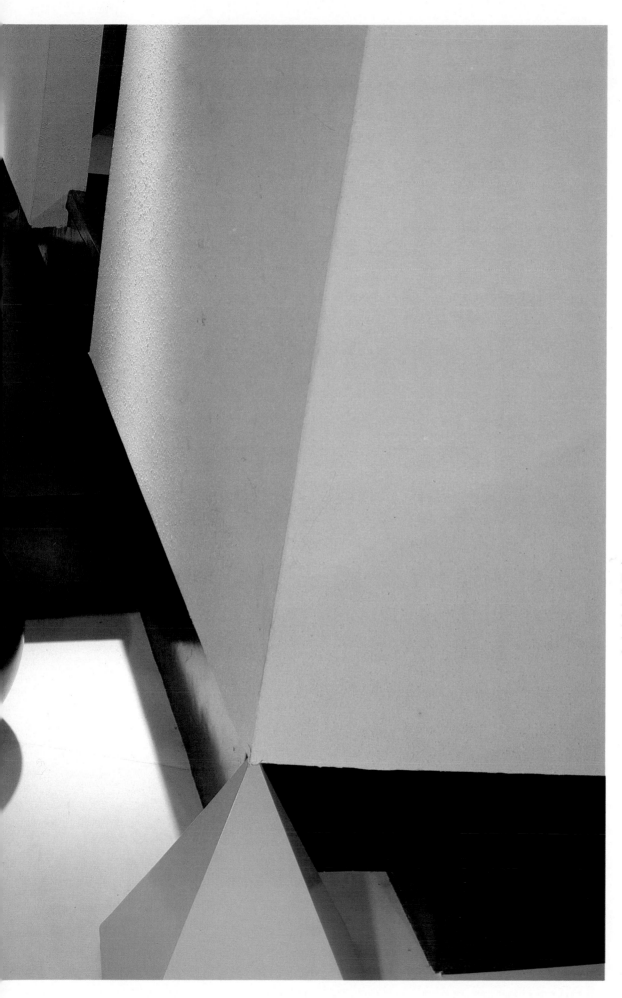

Tipping volumes on end,
Paul Haigh's witty
showroom for
Modern Mode,
designed in 1984,
was a personal semaphore
for the dislocation
of Modernism.

Clock in the Peter Cooper Suite at Cooper Union, New York, site of this book's Advisory Board meeting in 1988.

INTRODUCTION

The design of buildings, interior spaces, graphic communications, and consumer goods is the mirror of a society and its culture. The meaning of our lives is woven through everything we touch; the skyscrapers where we work, the homes in which we live, and even the throwaway cups from which, most often, we drink. American design expresses how this nation sees itself and where we, as a nation, think we are going.

Undertaking a review of American design between 1970 and 1990 is a bold task for a single mind. There is always the danger that personal taste, inclination, and friendship will present a biased perspective. This would not serve the public or history very well. To avoid such a potential hazard, editor Lois Brown and I invited twelve significant design leaders to form an advisory board that would provide input for this book. The members of this board were Kent Bloomer, Raul de Armas, Paul Haigh, Alexia Lalli, Michael McCoy, Margaret McCurry, Thom Mayne, Jeffrey Osborne, Ligia Ravé, David Slovic, Elizabeth Sverbeyeff, and Stanley Tigerman.

The group was carefully chosen so that no one design style or tendency—e.g., Modern, Post-Modern, Post-Industrial, Deconstructivism—would predominate. Also taken into consideration was each member's active involvement in the professions of architecture, interior design, and furniture design during the two decades under investigation. In addition, eight of the twelve have academic responsibilities in major schools of architecture and design.

In this cross-disciplinary context, the definition of "design," taken from *Webster's Third New International Dictionary*, is "a scheme for the construction, finish and ornamentation of a building as embodied in the plans, elevations and other architectural drawings pertaining to it," with its implied responsibility for the total concept, both inside and out, from the detailing of interior spaces to exterior form, fenestration, and facade. Supplementary definitions come from Francesco Baldinucci, who, in his *Vocabolario Toscano dell'arte del disegno* (1681), sees it as "a real demonstration of how forms of things come first from man's concept in his soul and imagination," and from John Thackara, a contemporary author and critic, who holds that design is a "planning process for the material world."

As a start, the advisory board convened for an all-day conference. This meeting, held in the Peter Cooper Suite of The Cooper Union in New York, proved to be an extraordinary lift-off for the publishing project. Two human recorders, Dominque Lalli and Nayana Currimbhoy, wrote down ideas as they surfaced and pinned them up on the wall. A tape recorder captured a total of 20,000 words in the eight hours of conversation.

It was a day that yielded a rich kaleidoscope of design history and wisdom. But the most interesting aspect of the experience was that these participants were insistent upon constantly juxtaposing the environmental design disciplines with the social and political context of the time. As Stanley

Tigerman pointed out, "Painting and sculpture are initiating acts of social and political commentary; architecture and design are responsive acts to the cultural landscape." Although many people outside the design milieu may suppose that design decisions are just a matter of creative or intuitive whim, a case was indisputably made by the advisory board that designers are likely, consciously or unconsciously, to weave reflections of contemporary cultural history into their work.

During the past two decades, design has captured the public's attention, and this interest does not stop at the home. Today, people are as conscious of public space design—the United Airlines terminal at Chicago's O'Hare Airport, Manhattan's Trump Tower, the Temporary Contemporary Museum in Los Angeles—as they are of the styles of master bedrooms and spa baths. The growing design-conscious society—resulting from affluent living, the two-income family, environmental issues, the preservation movement, and the feminist revolution, to name some prime factors—has transformed architecture from a remote and specialized profession into an everyday topic, even turning some architects into superstars who take their place next to Elizabeth Taylor in *People* magazine.

In the new AT&T Headquarters on Madison Avenue designed by Philip Johnson and John Burgee, the Golden Boy statue basks in a lobby of opulent marble and gold leafing.

The advisory board reviewed the period under investigation and, by consensus, identified four mainstreams of design: Historical Recall (Chapter 1: "As Times Go By"); Cybernetic Influence (Chapter 2: "Digital Dancing"); Deconstructionism (Chapter 3: "The Jaggered Edge"); and Process Design (Chapter 4: "We, The People"). It is not by accident that I decided to organize these four groups around musical references. Sonic rhythms are an original, basic human communication system, which, when harmonically coded, become music. Aural art forms, therefore—music and poetry—reach into people's consciousness much faster than any of the visual media, such as art and architecture. Society expresses moods and feelings through its music.

"AS TIMES GO BY," referencing the theme music from the movie classic *Casablanca* (still an all-time hit for its bittersweet nostalgia), outlines the inclination to incorporate historical icons as well as historical language innate to architecture into buildings, interiors, and furnishings. Over the last twenty years, the idea of the modern building, with its ennobling aspects of democratic simplification—bringing an interior space down to an open, free-flowing area suitable for universal tastes and lifestyles—has been eclipsed by a desire for historical recall that seems to span almost the entire spectrum of civilization, from the Egyptian pyramids to Greek temples, Renaissance villas, Gothic cathedrals, stately English homes and castles, and America's Western ranches. Ornament and decoration are layered into a building facade or interior—pediments, lintels, columns, vaulted ceilings and archways with trompe l'oeil, gold-and-silver leafing; frescoes, and moldings. There is no physical barrier to the application of these structural and decorative adornments. They can be employed in such diverse circumstances as corporate offices, fashionable restaurants, shopping malls, hotels, and Disneyland-type theme parks, as well as in the more lavish contemporary home. The interest in pastiche and collage as well as *profound* ornament, which is a fundamental aspect of what has come to be known as Post-Modern design, reflects, according to the advisory board, a relatively young nation intent on verifying its existence. Thus, faithful copying or (more often) the simulation of centuries-old historical motifs bestows a patina of sophistication. It helps to give the country the past that it never actually had.

"DIGITAL DANCING," summarizing the exhilaration of the computer revolution, lifting civilization off the planet to the stars, even beyond this universe (the theme of a piece of music written by rock star David Bowie in 1969), describes the process of linking up design with cybernetics, which has been somewhat slower than more technically oriented disciplines such as medicine, aerospace, and electronics. (The British design sensibility has forged ahead more progressively—with Richard Rogers' work at the Pompidou Centre in Paris and Norman Foster's in the Hong Kong and Shanghai Banking Corporation—but England has been a country of mechanical invention since the beginning of the Industrial Revolution.) Leading-edge technology—holograms, lasers, video, electronic synthesizers—is more often employed in the design of theme parks and discotheques than anywhere else. The high-tech minimal style is but a brave attempt to substitute industrial ready-mades for a future yet to come. But in the area of office design and automation, real changes have occurred, turning this industry into a $40 billion annual business within the last ten years. Office design for the "information society" is now a technical specialty requiring far more than tasteful aesthetics. What's needed is an understanding of the state of the art in computers, wiring, lighting, acoustics, telecommunications, and ergonomics—along with the spatial and psychological requirements of workers who are exposed to a totally new set of physical circumstances. Of all the happenings in the two decades under discussion, the advisory board concurred that the advent of microcomputer technology was probably the most important and most challenging to integrate into the design disciplines.

"THE JAGGERED EDGE," dealing with the aggressive tendency toward destruction and dislocation (and reflected in the music of numerous rock artists, who express a prevailing global chaos), is depicted in walls that are purposely peeling or torn away, in rough-textured interiors with bare concrete or cinder-block walls and "garage finished" floors, in jagged-edged furniture, bare-bulb lighting, and decorative elements that resemble broken shards. This has also been referred to as "anarchitecture" or "post-blast" design, the first being an attempt to dissolve established architectural canons, and the second a graphic interpretation of the world following the next nuclear holocaust. At its most sophisticated level, Deconstructionism is a conscious effort to translate the work of twentieth-century literary theorists—Jacques Derrida, Michel Foucault, and others who represent the Post-Structuralist linguistic philosophy—into built form. While some critics speak of the "poetics of the unfinished," the work creates an often brutal and disquieting aura. It can be perceived as a statement of anarchy, since it rebels against convention, and also as a message of the times, alluding to a world that is in the process of disintegration from environmental pollution and internecine conflicts. The advisory board did not regard this design tendency as a passing fad—some believed it was strongly rooted in prevailing social conditions and "serious."

"WE, THE PEOPLE," reflecting the more hopeful, optimistic signs of human interaction to solve global crises (as evidenced in the fund-raising rock festivals for African famine relief, AIDS, and Amnesty International), charts the efforts that are being made to bring about change within a new framework—the concept of hands-on Process Design. Its manifestations are seen in vigorous citizen involvement in shaping the urban and suburban landscape and cleaning up the indoor and outdoor environments. All over the country, local groups are taking action to achieve two goals: to preserve what twenty years ago would have been deemed of little or no value—old building stock of all kinds—and to make sensible, environmentally responsible community decisions for the generations to come. The nation is no longer in an era of new building but of rebuilding. Urban gardens and parks are being recovered from derelict corners of blighted cities, and in model neighborhoods—such as Davis, California—solar energy and recycling have helped the citizens to be independent of centralized bureaucracy. This is a new energy reacting to the disastrous "urban renewal" of the 1950s and 1960s, which razed existing structures and imposed monolithic megatowers in their place, taking away human scale and urban character without recourse to, or consideration of, people's actual needs. The advisory board emphasized the increasing need to involve the user in the design process. As David Slovic put it: "We should establish goals for architecture that articulate not the method or style of design but the use of design as a factor necessary to the improvement of society and its environment."

These four streams of design describe the main events of the past two decades as they are related to the social, political, and economic activities of this period. (They are not all-inclusive, however; lesser popular currents should not be dismissed, such as craft movements, regionalism, strict Modernism.) At the same time, the advisory board seemed to identify, overall, an optimistic direction for American society as it approaches the twenty-first century. The drive toward technology, while looking back at history, the urge to express the awful sense of global chaos, while trying actively to repair the situation, suggest that, in an increasingly uncertain world, there are strong currents directed toward improvement. With such a perspective in hand and hope in our hearts, we will travel into the third millennium with a basis for more intelligent and responsible actions toward a lasting society.

CHAPTER 1

Goodbye to all that. The dynamiting of the Pruitt-Igoe housing development in St. Louis on July 15, 1972.

You must remember this,

A kiss is still a kiss,

A sigh is just a sigh;

The fundamental things apply,

As time goes by.

The Pruitt-Igoe multistory housing complex in St. Louis, built between 1952 and 1955, was designed by world-class architect Minoru Yamasaki (who also designed New York's World Trade Center) and received an award by the American Institute of Architects. On July 15, 1972, it was demolished—reduced to a heap of rubble with tons of dynamite. The buildings, a series of high-rise concrete apartment blocks, had been part of a massive urban-renewal process. The intention was to house middle- and low-income families in modern apartments and, by so doing, impose order on apparently disorderly lives. But after twenty years the complex had been such a failure—with muggings in its corridors as well as graffiti, garbage, and drug dealing in the stairways—that local authorities felt they had no choice but to blast it to bits and start over.

It was a major media story around the world. What, the commentators asked, went wrong with the concept of housing people in concrete high rises? And what could be learned from the St. Louis mistake so that, in the future, hundreds of thousands of taxpayer dollars need not be spent to shelter citizens in environments they could not respect? They did not have to look far to find well-reasoned explanations. Philosophers such as Ivan Illich, Hannah Arendt, and E. F. Schumacher—as well as city planners such as Jane Jacobs—had already published arguments that countered the value of "rational" substitutes for traditional patterns. Efficient slab buildings with "streets in the air" safe from cars—but not, it turned out, safe from crime—lacked human scale and the feeling of "home." The repetitious monotony of apartment after apartment, with no marked features to distinguish one from another, affected the tenants' attitudes and feelings. They did not respond to a "clean" hospital metaphor; they simply did not feel good about living in vertically stacked, gray, flat-roofed egg crates. And who could blame them?

The architecture of the Modern school of design—also known as the International Style because of its transnational application—grew from a belief on the part of designers and planners that a society moving toward increasing equality and opportunity for all called for uniform planes and simple geometry. Expressions of economy and spareness signaled a departure from social hierarchy, wealth, and luxury for the fortunate few. With this in mind, decorative rooflines symbolizing crowns were rejected in favor of the flat-topped, unadorned surfaces that characterized Pruitt-Igoe. In its most successful implementations, the Modern approach had produced the shimmering glass tower of the United Nations Headquarters building and the elegant Museum of Modern Art in New York City. But unfortunately the simplicity of the design form had given rise, all across America, to thousands of less distinguished clones, which came down to nothing more than ugly concrete-and-glass boxes. Not only were these buildings boring to look at, but it was hard to tell the difference between a school, a bank, and a

Less is a bore? The 1939 Museum of Modern Art, New York, expressed the skeletal construction and reductive rules of Modern architecture.

Learning from Las Vegas, the automotive culture, and vernacular buildings, Robert Venturi praised the ugly and the ordinary in his 1972 manifesto.

Venturi's work progressed from the 1971 Trubek-Wislocki houses (*top*), set by the shore like vernacular fishermen's shacks, to the 1983 Wu Hall, Princeton (*center left*), reflecting, in its brick and fenestration, the Ivy League campus's history. His classical-style addition (*center right*) to the National Gallery in London, fits into the context of the existing building. In the Venturi's own home (*bottom*) in Philadelphia, more is obviously more.

motel. Rigid uniformity had destroyed idiosyncratic characteristics; regional and neighborhood familiarity had been bulldozed away in the name of "good" design for the "modern" era.

By the 1970s, the failure of this design philosophy was evident, not only by the devastating example of Pruitt-Igoe but in the sudden urge to produce hand-built houses, often with solar energy and recycled materials that enabled the occupant to opt out of the "official" system. And it was clear that America was changing. Opposition to the Vietnam War as well as support for the feminist revolution, black power, and gay rights ushered in a more open life-style and a reordering of priorities. In the wake of widespread sociopolitical unrest (such as the open revolt against the Brutalist style of the Modern Art and Architecture Building at Yale University, designed by architect Paul Rudolph, which students protested imposed an undesirable kind of "order"), the American design community looked for a new direction in favor of a truly American approach to design. It looked beyond the International Style and its heroes—Mies van der Rohe, Walter Gropius, and Marcel Breuer—all Europeans who had escaped from Nazi Germany to establish new careers and reputations in the United States between 1930 and 1960. From the rubble of Pruitt-Igoe, new ideas, new names, and also new buildings emerged.

From Philadelphia came the voice of Robert Venturi, a renegade but thoughtful architect. The failure of Modernism, Venturi claimed, stemmed from an elitist attitude that arbitrarily defined design as either "good" or "bad." There *was* no good or bad, he insisted. "It is from the everyday landscape, vulgar and disdained, that we can draw the complex and contradictory order that is valid and vital for our architecture as an urbanistic whole." His philosophy was expressed in a manifesto published in 1966 by the Museum of Modern Art, titled *Complexity and Contradiction in Architecture,* to be followed by *Learning from Las Vegas* in 1972 (authored by Venturi with his wife Denise Scott Brown and associate Steven Izenour), published by the MIT Press. Venturi lionized the "ugly and the ordinary"—the iconography of the "strip" and suburbia. They were rich in symbolism and decoration, he pointed out, and expressed what most people liked and reacted to positively. He found the giant billboards and neon signs of Las Vegas to be as symbolic of the twentieth century as the piazza was of ancient Rome. It was time to respond to the facts of life, the Venturi team said; speed, mobility, superhighways, and supermarkets were the realities of America today.

This radical point of view was not exactly what many designers were ready to hear, but Venturi nevertheless became the standard-bearer for a new vision, designing buildings that looked "normal" and "familiar," houses that fitted into their suburban or seaside context, apartments and public buildings that suggested on the outside their use on the inside. Yet as the Venturi firm grew and developed ideas in specific design commissions, it appeared that its homage was less to the present

Yale's Art and Architecture building by Paul Rudolph opened in 1963 to much student protest.

than to a romantic past of eighteenth-century Chippendale and Robert Adam, even referring to the Italian Renaissance and ancient Greece. While such historical references were sometimes linked to the architecture surrounding a Venturi project and reflected his desire to "fit into context" rather than stand out obtrusively, the retracing of past centuries was also perhaps a debt to Jean Labatut, Venturi's teacher at Princeton, who had been educated at the École des Beaux-Arts in Paris. The principles of this school, which dates back to 1789, are based on integrating art, ornament, and classical symmetry in the design of buildings. The 1909 suburban Philadelphia home of the Venturis—with its stenciled decoration around the walls and the mingling of graceful antiques from varying periods—was a visual clue as to where their tastes lay—in the historical continuum of design.

Another architect in New York who embraced the romantic tradition was Robert A. M. Stern, a professor of architecture at Columbia University. Launching into a series of vernacular-style houses in the early 1970s in the Hamptons on Long Island, New York, Stern brought back shingles, pitched roofs, gables, eyebrow windows, Palladian doors, and other familiar details absent in the Modern, white-painted, abstract structures that dotted the nearby shoreline. There was no denying that Stern's houses fitted into their context and could not be mistaken for anything other than gracious homes. Their historical design references implied stability and means. This was the kind of language people understood—ornamentalism that allowed the viewer to see a building as a building, without the overlay of intellectual or political connotations that had been the burden of Modernism. These houses elicited emotional rather than cerebral responses. And their interiors were comfortable and colorful, with window seats and niches, pastel silk fabrics, and antique rugs. Their owners were allowed to furnish them with their favorite family heirlooms rather than with the stark, modern furniture that characterized the austere, abstract Modern homes. The overall effect expressed a sharp change in visual appreciation. For those now "old school" Modern architects and interior designers, this was as much a shock as when Venturi compared the Las Vegas "strip" to the Roman Forum!

Architectural history was very much in the mind of Michael Graves, another young professor of architecture. He had been schooled in Modernism at the University of Cincinnati and was building small additions to houses in that style. But since 1962, when he joined the faculty at Princeton, he had been absorbing the Jean Labatut–École des Beaux-Arts legacy. He began producing architectural drawings, murals, and furniture that recalled Beaux-Arts ideas. Columns, pediments, colonnades, arches, and vaulted ceilings became part of Graves' new work, most of which was, at first, purely theoretical, since there were not many clients around who were able to understand it. As for materials and finishes, he proposed marble, inlaid wood, lacquer, and even gold leafing. Word got around and soon hundreds

The Ecole des Beaux-Arts philosophy bound classical symmetry and ornament.

Robert Stern's graceful beach cottage (*top and bottom*) on Long Island, designed in 1979, is influenced by surrounding turn-of-the-century homes. Furnishings in Stern's 1981 Mill Neck residence are comfortable and familiar.

Opposite page: Lyrical murals by Michael Graves for Princeton's John Witherspoon School and Jersey City's Liberty State Park introduce a vocabulary derived from the Beaux-Arts.

29

of students looking for a new messiah, given the demise of International Style Modernism, crowded into his lectures. He drew on traditional patterns, suggesting in one talk, titled "A Chest of Drawers," that anything from a bookcase to a high-rise building must have a bottom, a middle, and a top, like a sensible piece of furniture. These were the inescapable fundamentals, he said, and he used classical painting and religious iconography to illustrate his points. He gave new sanctity to "rooms," praised the processional route of corridors and the ceremonial aspects of hallways, and emphasized the importance of entrances—deifying the door, which, during the Modernist period, had been lost within the skin of the wall.

Meanwhile, at the Institute for Architecture and Urban Studies in New York, a new forum was established—in part by architectural eminence Philip Johnson (who, as a young curator at the Museum of Modern Art in 1932, had introduced the International Style to America)—to discuss the new directions in architecture and design. Fellows and their professional colleagues were formulating the language for what was clearly emerging as a major change. The generally agreed-upon umbrella title for the code was Post-Modernism. This term had first been used by architectural historian Nikolaus Pevsner in 1966 and was subsequently employed by Charles Jencks, a young critic, to encompass "trends which go counter to orthodox Modernism." Three broad principles were defined to identify Post-Modernism:

ORNAMENTALISM. The layering of meaning onto an exterior or interior with familiar references in texture or color. A typical Venturi building could be constructed of different-colored brick or have a facade of colored tile. In interiors, the rule "white is right" was discarded in favor of colored hues of paint, stenciling, and even wallpaper. This ran absolutely counter to the Modernist creed, which declared all extraneous detailing to be unnecessary and inappropriate, and espoused a preference for forthright and basic materials—concrete and glass.

CONTEXTUALISM. The careful observation of the buildings surrounding a proposed new structure and an effort to integrate the new with the old without being precisely faithful to existing history. This was typified by Stern's shingle houses, which sought to fit into the existing landscape of turn-of-the-century shingle cottages. This, again, ran absolutely counter to the Modernist creed, which vehemently dissociated itself from the past and proclaimed a new order by design statements. Marcel Breuer's Whitney Museum of American Art in New York was a classic example of this philosophical attitude. As an abstract concrete monolith, it struck out against the architectural heritage of Madison Avenue.

ALLUSIONISM. The positive attempt to define the use of the building by its design. This was expressed in the regional flavor of Venturi's vernacular beach houses in Martha's Vineyard, similiar in scale and appearance to the existing fishermen's shacks around them. Again, this ran absolutely counter to the Modern-

Demonstrating the value of the haptic and the syncretic, the Wonder Wall at the New Orleans Expo in 1984—by Charles Moore, Perez Associates, and Kent Bloomer—was a crowd pleaser.

ist creed, which designated a reductive and generic typology for all structures. Allusionism meant that the glass or concrete box, for all its elegant simplicity, was not the ideal universal structure. Variety was to be applauded, not deplored.

By 1978, there was enough substance to the theory of Post-Modernism for the Museum of Modern Art in New York to recognize formally what was happening. A major exhibition on nineteenth-century Beaux-Arts buildings was mounted as a blockbuster event, under the direction of architecture curator Arthur Drexler, suggesting that the design path ahead was firmly rooted in the past. Hard-core Modernists were clearly shaken by the news, but the message was heard. In that same year, Stanley Tigerman, leader of the Chicago Seven, a group of architects who were eager to show that not all the new ideas were coming from the East Coast, produced a collage called *The Titanic*. It was a drawing of one of Mies van der Rohe's most famous Chicago buildings, the Illinois Institute of Technology, going down at sea. This was coupled with a letter to Mies (who had taught the Modernist credo at that school for twenty years, between 1938 and 1958) citing "strange" things that were going on in design today—a nightclub with classical columns, a piazza in New Orleans with a wall spouting water.

The much-documented Piazza d'Italia in New Orleans, with its classical Roman detailing, was the work of architect Charles Moore, who reported his loss of confidence in Modernism in a seminal book—*Body, Memory and Architecture* (1977)—coauthored with his Yale University friend and colleague Kent Bloomer. It helped to establish new ways of looking at design that would respond to people's needs. Bloomer and Moore drew parallels between the physiographical characteristics of people and buildings, noting that a freestanding house with a back and front (body), an empty-space attic at the top (mind), a fireplace and hearth (heart), and a lower basement (implication of the id) asserts the typical American identity. Reaching back into history, they noted that columns were celebrations of the special human ability to assume an upright stance. Walls proclaimed territoriality. Roofs, even though obviously practical for shelter, served as crowns. These were fundamental concepts in the evolution of humankind. Four columns holding up a roof or four poles holding up a network of thatch or even a piece of cloth formed the basic pavilion, common for millennia as a place of celebration or worship. Christian churches had been built in the shape of the cross for symbolic reasons, their domes signifying heaven. In some ancient cultures, triangular pediments over doorways indicated a head man. In short, numerous codes in design were layered with more meaning than perhaps we were prepared to recognize. (While symbolisms had been handed down from generation to generation, oral explanations had been lost in the onward march of civilization.)

The Bloomer and Moore hypothesis introduced two key words: *haptic* and *syncretic*. "Haptic" expresses a system in

Going down. The IIT building by Mies van der Rohe in a seminal 1978 cartoon by Stanley Tigerman.

Roman orgy. The 1978 Piazza d'Italia in New Orleans by Perez Associates and Charles Moore drew backsplash for its quasi-historical allusions.

which the sense of touch is reconsidered to include the entire body. It incorporates sensations: pressure, warmth, cold, pain. "Syncretic" implies a collage-like layering of decoration that, while full of complexity and tradition, is not "above the heads" of ordinary people. The overall intention of incorporating both these ideas was to reorder priorities in design. The purpose of design should not be to produce an object, they said, but to create the feeling derived from the object—whether it is a house, with its rooms having an air of happy domesticity, or a chair, with its aspects of physical support and comfort. In their quest for more humanization of design, Bloomer and Moore even found bodily connections with the Beaux-Arts school. A good Beaux Arts plan, they declared, "is like a well-muscled body. Walls thicken to perform feats of support." A few years later, they were to collaborate on one of the most adventurous walls ever to be seen, the Wonder Wall at the 1984 New Orleans Expo, which combined the haptic with the syncretic, not to mention the humorous and playful. It became the icon of the Expo, conveying a sense of Disneyland, which undoubtedly drew the crowds.

It took a businessman with a sense of showmanship to seize upon the value of all these disparate but connected ideas circulating in the design world at the end of the 1970s. Robert Cadwallader, vice chairman of the SunarHauserman furniture firm and previously president of Knoll, hired Michael Graves to create a series of furniture showrooms in New York, Los Angeles, Chicago, Dallas, and Houston. The Los Angeles showroom opened in 1980. It was Graves' first opportunity to express his new, decorative Post-Modern style, and it was to have momentous repercussions for both designer and client. Sunar-Hauserman became the talk of the design community and emerged from relative obscurity to challenge the most illustrious names in the furniture business, such as Herman Miller and Knoll. And Michael Graves became an overnight media star. Big commissions rolled in, including a public-service building in Portland, Oregon, and the headquarters of the Humana Corporation in Louisville, Kentucky. These were to be followed by the addition to the Whitney Museum in New York and the Shiseido health club in Tokyo. Graves was named *Interiors* magazine's Designer of the Year in 1981, and with this honor came the burden of being the initiator of a new tendency. Much as misguided copyists had misinterpreted Modernism, others now seized on Graves' work as the cultural expression of a new era. Post-Modernism, or Po-Mo in the popular language used by critics and the media, was evaluated as a palette of dusky pink, mauve, blue, terra-cotta, and celadon out of the Italian Tuscan countryside, with columns and pediments and other classical motifs drawn from Graves' inspirations, the Palladian and Renaissance villas. Because the vocabulary was not difficult to emulate, it turned up in everything from hairdressing salons to boutiques, restaurants, and even smart doctors' offices as well as in the houses and apartments of the wealthy

Po-Mo by Michael Graves. Below, the 1980 Los Angeles SunarHauserman showroom; 1982 Humana headquarters, Louisville; 1982 Portland Civic Building. Opposite page (*top and center*), schemes for a hotel and convention complex at Disneyland, for completion in 1990, and (*bottom*) third version, done in 1988, of a proposed addition to New York's Whitney Museum.

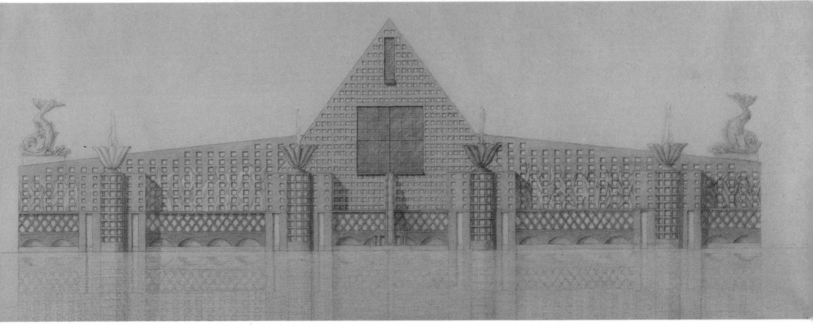

and fashionable. To be sure, the vocabulary contained the three cardinal principles of Post-Modernism, but simplistic interpretation substituted cosmetics for history and memory.

First published in 1977 in Great Britain, Charles Jencks' book *The Language of Post-Modern Architecture* attempted to convey the wide-ranging manifestations of the idiom, listing Historicism, Straight Revivalism, Neo-Vernacular, Urbanist Ad Hoc, Metaphor Metaphysical, and Post-Modern Space. It was seen that these examples ranged all the way from authentic re-creations of historical architecture and design to outrageous commentaries on the need for an architectural alternative to Modernism—expressed in buildings like Cesar Pelli's Pacific Design Center in Los Angeles, which was soon described as "The Blue Whale" because of its cumbersome and colorful marine-like lumpishness. However, it was the less profound nostalgic aspect of Post-Modernism that came to represent the genre.

Disneyland and the all-American icons Mickey and Minnie.

Scholars such as Stanley Tigerman explained the phenomenon with a two-point rationalization. The allusions to the past might be expressive, he said, of a search for identity in contemporary American society. In the face of lost wars in Korea and Vietnam, there was perhaps a fundamental need to look back to former wisdom, victory, and glory. Design canons that help to elicit these memories provide a cover of dignity and a sense of worthiness. In this sociopolitical context, these painful military defeats, previously unknown in the American experience, meant a loss of something more—the self-confidence that had characterized Modernism. The effort to find renewal in the past indicated that the nation was striving to verify its roots and foundation—which was, in effect, searching for a nonexistent past. The reversion to times gone by may be a way of acquiring the background and identity that this country has never had. It was an evaluation that struck a chord of sense. Equally plausible was the suggestion that since all of this historical playback is not truly authentic, it may also represent a measure of escapism. Americans, inventors of numerous synthetic products from movies to artificial fibers, have always enjoyed the world of "let's pretend." This is seen in the success of Disneyland, with its turreted seven-eights-scale castles and facades that recall Hamelin and the Pied Piper or scenes of the Wild West. These make-believe settings play on childhood fantasies. Significantly, when Michael Eisner, the new chief of the Disney empire, cast about in 1987 for a designer to create a business conference center next to the Orlando theme park, he chose Michael Graves, who then proceeded to ever-higher levels of fantasy with a hotel complex in the form of dolphins and swans.

The urge to simulate was evident in the twelve classical figures astride a new San Francisco high rise by Philip Johnson and partner John Burgee, who had them fashioned not in stone but of stiffened fabric. And the "Roman" columns in so many fashionable restaurants were commonly made of painted wood or plasterboard rather than marble. Unashamedly bogus, in some ways mocking the desire to reflect yesterday in today, they allowed for a skewing of the real and unreal, just like the game of "let's pretend." One upshot of this design-as-drama was that exhibition designers, accustomed to creating more transient settings, were suddenly busy in the interior design field. They were able to "stage-manage" Post-Modern products in appropriate backgrounds, whether in environments for advertising, photography, or display. One who achieved this with spectacularly successful results was Michael Vanderbyl, a San Francisco graphic designer working with Orlando Diaz-Azcuy's product designs for Hickory Business Furniture.

As the 1980s roared along, shrewd developers saw ways to capitalize on the prevailing mood and leaped onto the historical bandwagon. Trump Tower—designed by Der Scutt, then at the firm of Swanke Hayden Connell—signaled the revival of a bygone style that reiterated Scott Fitzgerald and the Jazz Age, with its lavish marble atrium, designer-shop arcades, piano player in tuxedo in the foyer, and doormen dressed in fancy uniforms copied from London. The environment begged shoppers to live it up—and they did! The Trumps themselves, Donald and Ivana, did the same, making their New York home in the tower's penthouse triplex, with its 80-foot living room. This, if not the world's biggest, was at least larger than any the Trumps had known.

Trump's colleagues soon learned that history paid off. Higher rents were to be gained by commissioning top architects to design in the Post-Modern style. Views of new, glamorous buildings even made existing buildings more valuable. It all translated into bigger profits. Gerald Hines, a Texan developer, embarked on a series of eleven high-rise buildings from coast to coast, with Philip Johnson and John Burgee as his architects. Turning away from the pure glass-curtain-wall boxes that he had designed so successfully for forty years, Johnson now drew to a different tune, borrowing romantically from the past—an Art Deco spire for the Transco building in Houston, gabled roofs from the Netherlands for the Republic Bank in Houston, and Gothic-style flying buttresses for the interior of this bank. For New York, Hines and Johnson produced the oval "lipstick" building at 53rd Street and Third Avenue, so called because of its pink marble cladding and its shape, somewhat reminiscent of 1930s ocean-liner design, with an overscale triumphal archway in the lobby and a columned arcade on the surrounding sidewalk. For other developers and corporate clients, Johnson and Burgee indulged wholeheartedly in gold leafing and intricate marble veneers, the more luxe the better. The executive floors of the Chippendale highboy-topped AT&T building on New York's Madison Avenue, done with interior designers Louis Beal and Joseph Rosen, were linked by an extraordinary white Carrara marble stairway, with balustrade and railing in marble to boot. For his own domestic quarters, Johnson pursued the path away from the Modernist

Glitz galore. The Trump Tower atrium, six floors of razzle-dazzle and water wall by Swanke Hayden Connell's design principal Der Scutt. Ivana and Donald Trump set a new style for conspicuous design in the 1980s.

motto "less is more" to the Post-Modern slogan embraced by Venturi: "less is a bore." Accordingly, next to the 1949 transparent glass box that had been the most famous and most photographed home of its time, he built a stucco guest house and art museum with vaulted ceilings and other architectural intricacies.

But it was in the area of hotel design that some of the most extravagant historical statements were conceived. West Coast designer Charles Pfister worked on the Grand Hotel in Washington, D.C., with a theme straight out of the 1919 Beaux-Arts Plaza Athenée Hotel in Paris. A graceful marble-floored rotunda served as the check-in reception area, a grand colonnaded allée led into the lounges and restaurants, while French floor-to-ceiling glass doors opened out onto a terrace garden. Leona and Harry Helmsley had no wish to portray their hotels as anything other than re-creations of plush European palaces, over which Mrs. Helmsley (the queen) could stand guard. Interior designer Sarah Tomerlin Lee (with architects Hardy Holzman Pfeiffer) spent years on the restoration of the famous Willard Hotel in Washington, D.C., with its turn-of-the-century Victorian detailing, while also executing the elegant Le Meridien Hotel in New York, with its ornate marble and tapestry settings. Working with architects Jung/Brannen for a client in Florida, she drew up plans for the interior of an extravagant health spa designed as a complex of Palladian-style villas. Mrs. Lee furnished the forty-five suites and treatment facilities on a budget of $32 million; her purchases included a 1920s Art Deco staircase designed by Jacques-Emile Ruhlmann, which she found languishing in a warehouse and acquired for $1 million. Artists were called in to create murals; marble was lavished on the floors; silks, tapestries, and chandeliers reigned in the restaurants.

The retracing of the past left some famous firms in a dilemma. Skidmore, Owings & Merrill had built its reputation on design that epitomized the clean, bare-bones style of Modernism. Their notable achievements included the award-winning Lever House of 1950, which was declared a historic landmark in 1986. But the forty-four partners realized they could not successfully serve clients without diversifying their range. As Partner in Charge of Interiors Raul de Armas put it: "We must find another octave." With Associate Partner Davis Allen, he proudly did a retrofit of the Manufacturers Hanover Bank headquarters in New York, taking it from 1950s spare and sleek to 1980s new Baroque. Its octagonal pavilions veneered in marble, museum-quality antiques, and sumptuous silks and damask would be enough to make Louis XVI feel at home. The Skidmore approach to clients was to cushion the effects of an increasingly technological working environment. Although it had been predicted that upper management would never be enslaved to monitors and keyboards, there was hardly a CEO who was not on line only five years after the advent of the personal computer. De Armas took the utilitarian aspect of PCs

Opposite page: In the clouds. Skyscrapers by Philip Johnson and John Burgee are loosely derived from Chippendale (*top*), Flemish traditions, transatlantic liners, and Art Deco (*center*). Johnson's 1980 stucco building (*bottom*) contrasts strongly with his famous 1949 Glass Box—both on his estate.

Octagonal lobbies in the refurbished offices of Manufacturers' Hanover Trust, by Raul de Armas of Skidmore, Owings & Merrill, recall Andrea Palladio.

away by housing them in lavish, custom-fabricated cabinets that Thomas Jefferson would have appreciated.

This day and age we're living in gives cause for apprehension
With speed and new invention and things like third dimension
We get a trifle weary with Mister Einstein's theory
So we must get down to earth, at times relax, relieve the tension
No matter what the progress, or what may yet be proved
The simple facts of life are such they cannot be removed.

These lyrics from a verse of the song from *Casablanca*, written in 1931, not quite as well known as the chorus, spoke to a concern that was obviously threatening the electronic generation. The design solution for those less able to cope with the swift onslaught of microchips was to shroud the automated office in familiar packaging. Probably most illustrative of this strategy was the great new headquarters complex for the Equitable Life Assurance Society on New York's West Side.

With architect Edward Larrabee Barnes as its designer (the Modernist who built the sleek IBM tower on 57th Street in New York), it started off as a classically Modern granite-and-glass tower with a flat roof. And then Chairman of the Board John Carter, reflecting the signs of the times, called in the interior design firm of Kohn Pedersen Fox Conway to give Post-Modern Jeffersonian touches to the interiors. Historical extravagances included a forty-foot vaulted ceiling in the multicolumned board room and dining room, located on the fiftieth floor. KPFC's modifications to the original building enabled a great spread of windows on both the east and west elevations to enhance these interior spaces, a shift that dramatically changed the look of the tower as it met the skyline. In keeping with the Monticello vocabulary were the typical work stations, custom-made with mullioned glass windows and classical moldings for clerical and middle-management employees. Patricia Conway, the partner in charge of the Equitable project, led a team of colleagues into a new experience of grand office interiors. There were four working fireplaces, a music room, and thirteen private dining rooms that captured the essence of the prevalent historical revival.

The ripple effect of Post-Modernism, as the 1980s came to a close, was evident across the country, from pediments and colonnades in neighborhood shopping malls to the careful (and sometimes not so careful) copies of eighteenth-century Georgian homes that became the standard model for builder homes and condominiums. In 1932, Le Corbusier, one of the founders of Modernism, had offered the challenge "architecture or revolution." In 1987, the prolific Charles Jencks, by now author of half a dozen books, revised his perspective of the design happenings from 1960 to 1985 into four traditions: Fundamentalist Classicism, Revivalist Classicism, Urbanist Classicism, and Eclectic Classicism. He maintained that "We are still near the beginning of the classical phase, and although one cannot predict its

Opposite page: Backward looks in Washington, D.C., at the Grand Hotel (*top*), with interior by Charles Pfister in the style of the 1919 Beaux-Arts Plaza Athenée in Paris. In Coral Gables, Florida, the Saturnia Health Spa (*center and bottom*) with architecture by Jung/Brannen and interiors by Sarah Tomerlin Lee in the style of Italian Renaissance villas.

History repeats itself at the Equitable Life Assurance New York offices—designed by Kohn Pedersen Fox Conway Associates—with echoes of Thomas Jefferson's Monticello.

future, it is likely to deepen as it synthesizes the distant and more recent past, as it sustains more profoundly the western tradition of humanism." In our fast-paced, multimedia, communications-driven era, the common yearning for a time when life was more gracious, more livable, and more human will propel an increasing taste for historical revival, or historic "truth" through recall and discovery.

CHAPTER 2

The dichotomy of urban
development progress
results in trash overload.

Ground control to Major Tom,

Ground control to Major Tom:

Take your protein pills and put your

helmet on.

Ground control to Major Tom:

Commencing countdown, engines on.

Check ignition and may God's love be

with you.

This is ground control to Major Tom;

You've really made the grade!

And the papers want to know whose shirts

you wear.

Now it's time to leave the capsule if you

dare.

This is Major Tom to ground control;

I'm stepping thro' the door,

And I'm floating in a most peculiar way.

And the stars look very different today.

In 1972, a dramatic exhibition called "Italy: The New Domestic Landscape" opened at the Museum of Modern Art, New York. It was organized by Emilio Ambasz, the curator of design, and took modern design off in a new direction. It had been a long-standing assumption of the Modern movement, according to Ambasz, that if all of humanity's products were well designed, harmony and joy would reign eternally triumphant. But, of course, there were signs from many different sources that "good" design is not in itself sufficient to ensure the solution to human problems (see Chapter 1).

"The New Domestic Landscape" was notable because it introduced a dimension beyond aesthetics, focusing on a concern for the aesthetic of the uses to which an object is to be put. Thus, said Ambasz, "the object (from the spoon to the city) is no longer conceived as an isolated entity, sufficient unto itself, but rather as an integral part of the larger natural and sociocultural environment." A confluence of circumstances provided an opportunity for designers to investigate larger issues of contemporary life. Massive urban decay and increasing population density worldwide (the United Nations predicted half the world's people would be city dwellers by the year 2000); poverty; inflation; the energy crisis; pollution of air, earth, and water; and a consumer society oriented to reckless waste were causing critical concern. At the same time, the revolution in technology and communications, the possibilities offered by new hard and soft synthetic materials and advanced molding techniques, as well as extended cross-cultural exchange made possible by the global expansion in airplane travel, provided inspiration and solutions.

New on the domestic landscape in 1972, molded plastic chairs by Vico Magistretti for Artemide.

The MoMA show demonstrated how designers could provide low-cost, comfortable, easy-to-maintain furniture using the new molded plastics and polyurethane. The problem of ever-decreasing urban living spaces was addressed with mobile modular units that contained functional elements—kitchens, bathrooms, beds, closets, tables, desks, storage—to be pulled out and opened up as required, with integrated plumbing, electrical, and other technological gear, including stereo, telephone, ventilation, heating, lighting, cooling, television, and laundry machines.

These designs presented a fundamental break with living traditions. They disposed of the long-established notion that rooms should be equipped with fixed arrangements of furniture for one specific use—a bedroom, a living room, a dining room. These designs presented options for flexibility, making one room serve many functions. They allowed the user to make his or her own statement about both privacy and communality. And it was also possible to vary atmosphere—happy, romantic, mysterious—by rheostat lighting controls and stereo sound. While these furnishings were extraordinarily functional and made of high-tech materials, they had none of the austere, hard-edged, unfriendly, and uncomfortable feeling of furniture that was generally labeled "Modern." They tended to be curved and sensuous in shape and pleasant to the touch, whether in smooth, hard plastic or soft, squeezable foam. This new, sybaritic domestic landscape reflected the new social freedom of the times—the sexual revolution, which liberated men and women from restrictive codes of behavior, and the prevailing indulgence in mood-altering sensations, running all the way from mind-bending music to marijuana and beyond.

To be sure, the MoMA show confirmed the responsive nature of design as an activity. It came fifteen years after the first Sputnik was launched and thirty years after cybernetics—the study of human control functions and of mechanical and electronic systems designed to replace them—was introduced by Norbert Wiener. Indeed, descendants of the first Sputnik had gone on to other planets and were now exploring stars beyond the solar system. But the show recognized a renewed interest in current industrial technology and electronics and their inevitable influence on the future.

One result was that two journalists, Suzanne Slesin and Joan Kron, teamed up to produce a book called *High Tech* (1978)—a play on the words "high style" and "technology"—which was a consumer road map and resource guide to low-cost, off-the-rack industrial products. It became an instant "bible" for all those interested in creating a new kind of modern environment. In the book's foreword, Emilio Ambasz declared that resorting to found objects and ready-mades out of context represented a sort of moral protest for a future yet to come; he noted that a pioneer in this campaign had been Charles Eames, with his radical Santa Monica House built in 1949 from a compendium of found objects and ready-mades such as doors and windows, steel columns, and open-web joints normally used in the construction of factories. But still there was a captivating freshness about the concept of high tech, which departed from established design traditions. In the area of lighting alone there were so many possibilities—blue aeronautical runway lights used to illuminate a kitchen by designer Alan Buchsbaum; clamp-on photographic umbrella lights in a living room; and even a string of cheap construction-site lamps with bulbs and wire all exposed. Architect Paul Rudolph proposed tractor tires upholstered in sensuous stretch fabric for furniture; gym lockers and dry-cleaners' conveyor belts came into play as storage; steel scaffolding was employed to create mezzanine loft spaces.

The reach for an antiestablishment aesthetic was the counterpart of a new art movement. Some young artists and sculptors were exchanging traditional media—paint, stone, bronze—for computers, video screens, holograms, and lasers. Despite the disapproval of traditionalists, who insisted that "Digital Art" was a contradiction in terms, by the early 1970s some galleries were already showing cybernetic art. Video pieces by Nam June Paik, a young Korean based in New York, were fetching upwards of $10,000.

The New York interior and industrial designer Ward Ben-

Ad hoc high tech. The use of practical industrial materials in the Peter de Bretteville residence in California.

nett (who had apprenticed with Le Corbusier) was a formidable catalyst, drawing younger designers eager to develop the new aesthetic. As early as 1950 he had used a subway grating in a duplex apartment as part of a stairwell and oversize stainless steel hospital tubs in clients' bathrooms, with Con Edison guard rails for towel racks and theatrical "barn" lights in place of "standard" domestic fixtures. Bennett had a special genius for putting what had been looked upon as mundane industrial "blue-collar" items into refined and elegant settings: sisal matting for floors, butcher-apron linen for walls. The juxtaposition of economical choices was the hallmark of his work. One of Bennett's most inventive protégés was Joseph D'Urso, whose idiosyncratic control of space and clutter brought his talents into heavy demand among urban clients with limited living spaces. He transformed confining rooms into apparently limitless terrains. Through an ingenious use of partial walls, built-in furniture, raised platforms, and changing patterns of light, he achieved a singular spareness, startlingly empty of "things." Monotone compositions of black, white, and gray—most often accompanied by the use of track lighting, industrial blinds, skylights, hardware, mirrors, and carpeting—gave rise to a descriptive term he heartily disliked: high-tech minimalism. To counter this, he would point out that his designs depended heavily on expensive hand-craftsmanship. But it was still true that he selected off-the-rack, nuts-and-bolts equipment—a dressing table, for instance, might be equipped with a supermarket detection mirror and a secretarial stool. Nevertheless, his vision attracted a specific kind of client, often someone who was on the threshold of a major personal change, even a transformation of existence, casting out the unnecessary, the sentimental, and the familiar in favor of a supremely contemporary, up-to-the-minute environment. (The social revolution encouraged divorce, singleness, and remarriage and provided the impetus for personal reevaluation.) Furthermore, D'Urso's sublimely poetic but stark, light-filled spaces were allied with bluntly real, low-maintenance materials such as wall-to-wall industrial carpeting as well as rubber and plastic surfaces that responded easily to the vacuum cleaner and the sponge.

By the end of the 1970s, the reductive and radical D'Urso aesthetic captured the attention of big business, bringing him a commission to design a blockbuster retail store in Los Angeles for the Esprit fashion enterprise. Here D'Urso's austere raw concrete building—with its interior punctuated by exposed steel beams, metal cables, and piping supporting a complexity of spotlights and industrial-looking metal clothes racks—was a reinforcement for the youthful New Age style of the store, which sold merchandise via videos and the blaring sound of rock music. The concept was copied in dozens of boutiques across the country.

Michael Kalil was another Ward Bennett protégé whose search for a new aesthetic resulted in reductive sculptural spaces. However, his work was based on complex mathematical

Laurie Anderson performs high-tech video art in this laser photograph by Nam June Paik.

Experiments with fabric-covered rubber tires (*opposite*) by Paul Rudolph, mirrored factory skylights (*top*) by Ward Bennett, and metal piping (*bottom*) by Joseph Paul D'Urso in the Esprit store, Los Angeles.

calculations blended with cybernetics. In 1978, he published a proposed design for a city apartment in which computers controlled a kinetic floor and earth, fire, and water were present as symbols of primitive needs. Kalil—trained in weaving, sculpture, engineering, architecture, interior design, and industrial design—forecast a new symbiotic relationship between the synthetic, intangible realm of information technology and the tangible forces of the natural world. They were moving closer together, he said, because the artificial simulation was steadily becoming more organic—a biological process as opposed to a mechanical one in its system of organization—nearer to the system within the human body. Kalil's moving floor allowed for numerous reconfigurations of furniture—benches, tables, and seats to be propelled robotically from underneath, as required. This concept had broader implications for the workplace, particularly the future space station orbiting the earth, where zero gravity and restricted living, working, sleeping, and recreational areas would require a single zone that could serve multiple functions.

In 1984, Kalil designed a prototype executive-office environment in which every aspect of the space was computer-controlled, from the door lock (a hand imprint implanted in the door and electronically sensitized to recognize the handprint of the office user) to the variable colors and light within the space, programmed by the individual user with a joystick, and activated by a heat sensor. A working cockpit was placed opposite three giant video screens, receiving information from the universe. The space was multifunctional, with furniture (bed, couches, tables, chairs) for sleeping, dining, or meetings designed like Japanese origami in a series of folding pieces. Rising and unfolding from under the kinetic floor, they returned there when not in use, to be stored in a space less than seven inches deep. A further dimension was introduced with provision for mind-to-mind thought transference, or ESP. "As we reach for a new experience of living and working, we will expand our ability to use the mind and transcend normal levels of earthly consciousness," Kalil explained. This project produced widespread repercussions, resulting in TV coverage, lectures all over the world, and a contract from NASA to create the first living quarters for astronauts in space stations.

While offices in reality were nowhere near as sophisticated as in Michael Kalil's proposal, nevertheless, throughout the decades of the 1970s and 1980s, the workplace became a new subject of focus and interest. The feminist revolution brought more and more women into the white-collar information and service industries, where their influence on workplace environment increased. Their strong preferences and feelings and their smaller physical frames demanded the rethinking of spaces, colors, and facilities. The rise of the electronic office, with its small personalized computers, caused one of the biggest shifts in the history of design. In terms of organizing the planning of a building, it was akin to the changes that had taken place when electric lighting and central heating systems were introduced. Designers suddenly became involved with a whole new function.

To express this technological progress, one designer in particular tried very hard to push the principles of Modernism into a new realm. In 1967, Helmut Jahn had immigrated to America from Germany to undertake graduate studies at the Illinois Institute of Technology in Chicago. Soon he joined the city's prestigious architectural firm of C. F. Murphy, and such was his talent that he rose to director of planning and design in 1973 and went on to become principal of the office, reorganized as Murphy/Jahn, in 1981. Jahn's buildings celebrated all that was new in construction materials, particularly glass. And their forms and colors were unexpectedly exuberant, seeming to reflect the Space Age. One in particular, which took six years to construct, was the State of Illinois Center, dubbed "Helmut's helmet" because of its asymmetrical, curving shape. It was a shimmering, glass-walled building that defined the urban grid and the context of the surrounding architecture. Its seventeen floors were capped with a tilted, cylindrical skylight. As a government building for office workers—with its light-filled atrium and gondola elevators whizzing up and down like space shuttles—it was utterly unique. Jahn's popularity increased enormously throughout the 1980s and commissions came from many cities, including New York, where he set up a satellite office to implement three major office towers. In his hometown of Chicago, he took airport design to a new level of the grand terminal—a gateway to the city with the United Airlines Terminal at O'Hare. "Architecture is not just a matter of being a dreamer and going in a corner and coming up with ideas," he said. "It is building to fit a particular need."

Reflection of the Space Age. The Illinois State Building by Helmut Jahn.

Up to the 1970s, the office was not exactly a top priority in the American corporate world. To be sure, there were a few pacesetters, such as IBM, Time Inc., and CBS, which were committed to the highest standards of design in every phase of their operations. But for the most part the average office environment was a dreary place, full of the types of desks that had been around since World War II. However, studies by Louis Harris and others helped corporate leaders realize that concern for employee comfort and well-being gave a return that surpassed salary compensation and bonuses.

The open "landscape" office for middle-management—with low, partitioned cubicles arranged around a "work station"—had been introduced in Germany in the 1930s without eliciting great enthusiasm. Most employees preferred individual, private offices and resented the "bullpen" type of setup. But with the increasing costs of real estate, ever-diminishing square footages, and the need to accommodate growing numbers of white-collar workers in the new service and information industries, designers and manufacturers refined the open office system to make it an attractive place in which to work. Herman Miller's Action Office, a forerunner designed by Robert Probst

Generation gap. The 1950s work environment (*opposite*) versus the 1980s work spaces by Michael Kalil: a kinetic-floored executive office (*top*) and a future space station for NASA (*bottom*).

in the 1960s, was quickly followed by those of other manufacturers in the 1970s and 1980s, until well over one hundred and fifty firms were offering variations. The vertical panels of these systems were designed with complex electronic capabilities, enabling them to cope with computers, telephones, modems, and lighting while also providing outlets for other gadgets such as calculators, printers, and even teakettles. The work-station concept deftly took care of the unsightly and hazardous spaghetti-like wiring associated with all this equipment. Refinements were made in detailing. Sound-masking insulated fabrics and white-noise systems installed in ceilings countered decibels, so that the individual work-station user could easily have private telephone conversations. Emilio Ambasz won design awards for a series of office spaces that paired high-tech functionalism with elegance, using strands of silk as dividing "screens" between work stations. And then came the ergonomic chair. In the new automated office, workers were exposed to a totally new set of physical circumstances, often being glued to computer screens and keyboards for many hours. Therefore, backaches, neck aches, and eyestrain became constant complaints. These problems demanded attention (see Chapter 4).

At the industrial design firm of Henry Dreyfuss in Los Angeles, comprehensive human-dimensions research had been done by Niels Diffrient in the late 1960s and early 1970s. A determination of physical proportions and seating requirements was needed for special situations such as automobile and airplane cockpits as well as wheelchairs for the infirm and elderly. In 1979, for Knoll, Diffrient introduced the first example of American adjustable office seating responding to individual human movements. A lever mechanism enabled the user to shift height and to lean back during rest periods, supporting the vulnerable lower back area. Later on, more sophisticated automatic versions let the chairs do the thinking, altering their angles and resistance as the user moved forward and backward, working and resting, twisting and turning approximately every eight minutes.

As the new information society took shape, other products were needed—such as storage for computer paper, floppy disks, and printouts. Carpet tiling was invented to enable new flat underfloor wiring to be installed and tapped into more easily than conventional broadloom carpeting would permit. Raised-access flooring allowed for cabling and the extra HVAC necessary for a room in which literally hundreds of computers might be humming, servicing journalists at *The New York Times* or traders at Merrill Lynch. And new finishes arrived, dispersing the buildup of electromagnetism (a threat to the efficient functioning of computer equipment and to human health) or dampening sound in spaces where high-speed printers were clattering. The office industry boomed, growing to an estimated $40 billion annual business by 1988.

Suddenly the office-building developers began speaking of "smart" or "intelligent" buildings, referring to the use of elec-

Opposite page: New tools for the information society. The typical computer work-station office (*top*) by Emilio Ambasz, made user-friendly with elegant silk dividers. The Diffrient chair (*bottom*), adjustable in height and back position.
The Vertebra chair (*below*) by Emilio Ambasz and Giancarlo Piretti, designed to adjust automatically with any movement of the body.

Terminal fever and instant global communication in the trading room at Merrill Lynch, designed by Raul de Armas at Skidmore, Owings & Merrill. Opposite, the phone industry revolution.

tronically enhanced and structurally advanced building design and construction. Office towers now had fiber-optic "data highways" running through walls as well as "talking" elevators and electronic "brains" to figure all the needs (heating, lighting, cooling) of the occupants in any given zone. (The earlier thermostats were as antiquated as 33 rpm phonograph records.) Walls were so airtight and insulated that dramatic savings in energy could be achieved in conjunction with windows that were regulated electronically to control solar gain.

Assets for owners, developers, and tenants were no longer measured only in tangible and visible examples of prosperity and wealth, such as lobbies detailed in marble and brass, but also in lucratively invisible and intangible elements related to technology. Even the siting and orientation of a structure to take advantage of solar energy could have a great impact on the heating and air-conditioning system operating within it. To avoid consumer legal actions and costly damage payments, it was essential to have systems that would monitor the health of the building, its air quality and bacteria count, as a cautionary strategy to prevent Legionnaire's disease and other ailments caused by circulating polluted air. Shared two-way interactive video teleconferencing increased the effectiveness of meetings while reducing travel expenses; these were tenant "perks" that justified higher rentals. Facility management, a new profession, interacted between designer, engineers, and contractors to make sure that all the telecommunications equipment—coaxial cable, twisted pair, LANs (local area networks), and PBXs (private branch exchanges)—were conducted to individual floors via cellular decks with a grid pattern of hollow wiring chases and channels cast right into the concrete floor slab. Interior furnishings were monitored for prescribed decibel levels, while materials were designed with antimicrobial, static-free, fire-resistant finishes. Reflectance factors were checked to determine the lighting levels in a given area and lamps measured for watts and footcandles per square foot.

Panasonic introduces a cordless telephone small enough to fit into your shirt pocket. And that's not even the big news.

In a condition that the French sociologist Jean Baudrillard calls an "ecstasy of communication," the 1980s saw portable briefcase-size computers become standard business equipment, facsimile transmission—FAX—grow within a year of its introduction to a $9 billion industry, automatic teller machines dispense cash on the street, and cellular car phones become as common as car tape decks and stereos.

The microchip generation spawned a whole new cadre of sci-fi "cyberpunk" writers who went far beyond Arthur C. Clarke and Isaac Asimov, now grandfathers of the genre. With his first novel in 1981, William Gibson, earning the sobriquet of cyberpunk's true prophet and protovisionary, described an eerie world of simulated stimulation ("simstim"); of "trodes" like Walkman headsets that enable the wearer to tap into and physically experience another person's "sensorium" anywhere in the world; of electronic black-market surgical facilities offering nerve implants to enhance response time, provide a whole new skin, or install a new personality when one tires of the old one; and of seemingly endless "spare parts" like those of an automobile service station. Even "serious" artists speculated on the future—for example, novelist Doris Lessing described the rivalries and interactions of great imaginary galactic empires in a series of novels written in the 1980s, teaming up with avant-garde composer Philip Glass to create an opera about mythical Canopus, Sirius, and its enemy Puttiora. The confirmation of a public captured by futuristic fantasies was clear from the stream of Hollywood movies that included *Star Wars, Star Trek, Close Encounters of the Third Kind,* and *Blade Runner.* The lurking suspicion of demonic control by an artificial intelligence—such as HAL in Arthur C. Clarke's legendary *2001*—waned with the lovable robot R2D2 in *Star Wars* and the grotesque but soulful extraterrestrial creature from outer space in *E.T.*

Despite this public enthusiasm, designers themselves—well behind professionals in medicine, aerospace, surface transportation, and electronics—were slow to take up Space-Age technology in their own work. In 1979, in the Westinghouse laboratories, where computer science had developed the know-how to get Americans orbiting in space, the concept of computer-aided design (CAD) was first demonstrated. In a darkened room with young "hackers" at computer terminals, visitors saw how design could be removed from the drawing board to the computer screen and subsequently transposed onto ultraprecise drawings created by high-speed laser-driven plotters. The drawings on the computer screen could be transposed into three dimensions at the press of a command key and erased and redrawn in the blink of an eye. Just as traditionalists criticized the use of computers to create art forms, conservative designers and architects similarly dismissed CAD as "purely mechanical." It would never replace the pencil and paper used since the days of Leonardo da Vinci as design tools. However, by the mid-1980s, the technology had advanced, so that it was possible to "walk through" a three-dimensional environment on the screen, turn it upside down, see it from a bird's-eye view at floor level, and consider it from more angles than it was possible to draw by hand. Software packages were written for lighting designers, so that they could simulate lighting effects and tell exactly where light and shadow would fall in a given space. This was a vast leap forward over the cardboard models used previously. Aside from using CAD for mechanical engineering calculations, space stacking, client furniture inventory, and business administration, many leading architectural and design firms were "selling" clients with computer-generated videos. They were creating entire city landscapes in computer graphics and moving through them as if in a low-flying aircraft, finally zooming in on the client's site and showing how their proposed buildings and interiors would look in relation to the surrounding environment. By 1987, the video presentation incorporating computer graphics was a standard requirement for most architectural competitions. And one adventurous designer, Gary Whitney, opening his new office in Houston, actually did away with drafting boards entirely. His six-person team, equipped with microcomputers and designing everything from furniture to condominium developments, landed commissions worth $1.5 million in their first nine months of operation—a staggering amount of work that could never have been accomplished by so few by traditional methods. The irony was that the work under construction used materials, techniques, and technologies familiar in building for centuries—stone, brick, and timber—and slightly newer materials from the nineteenth century: reinforced concrete and steel!

What was really needed, according to David Nixon and Jan Kaplicky, two future-oriented young architects with offices in Los Angeles and London, was a building revolution to pull designers through to the twenty-first century. They pointed out that the twentieth century had been a time of peak technological breakthroughs almost "indistinguishable from magic"—when the Wright brothers first demonstrated the feasibility of sustained flight; when the first Apollo astronauts stepped onto the surface of the moon; when the first home computer was announced by Apple; when a human life was first extended by the use of the Jarvik heart. But the building industry had remained virtually static for years! Any new inventions had been prohibitively expensive or difficult to employ. Working on experimental projects, Nixon and Kaplicky produced a series of provocative and inventive alternatives, including a kinetic living capsule mounted on the arm of a standard articulating hydraulic crane; a high-grade small-business building which, instead of conventional slab and foundations, used interlocking aluminum decking designed for emergency aircraft runways; and an arched enclosure system made of standard steel sand-

Spaced out. Multifunctional table unit for NASA crews in orbit, designed by David Nixon and Jan Kaplicky of Future Systems.

wich panels. Their NASA space station project included a multifunction table unit enabling eight people to dine or meet and adaptable living compartments for crew members. Their method was to engage spin-off technology from other disciplines—aviation, marine, automotive, and space engineering—"to help give energy to the spirit of architecture."

As the 1980s rolled to a close, stereolithography, a design breakthrough, came from a cybernetic engineer in California's

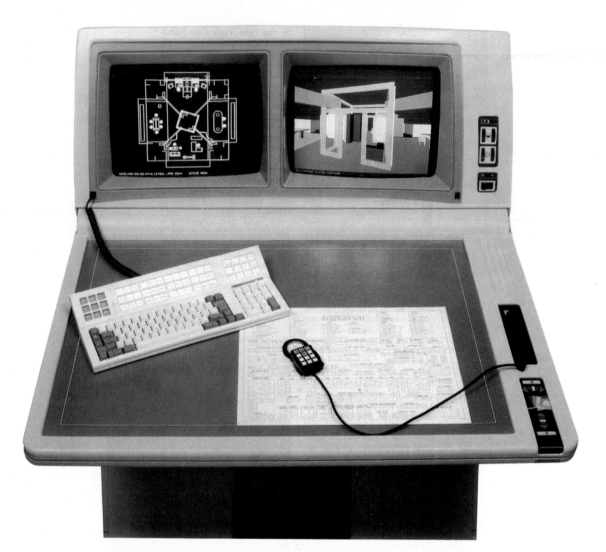

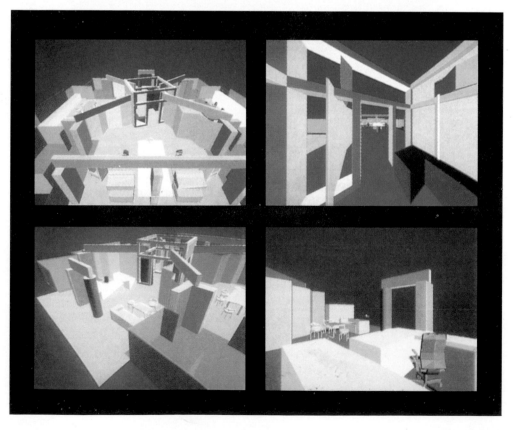

CAD at work. A design office planned by Cranbrook Academy students using computer-aided design equipment in a project directed by Michael McCoy.

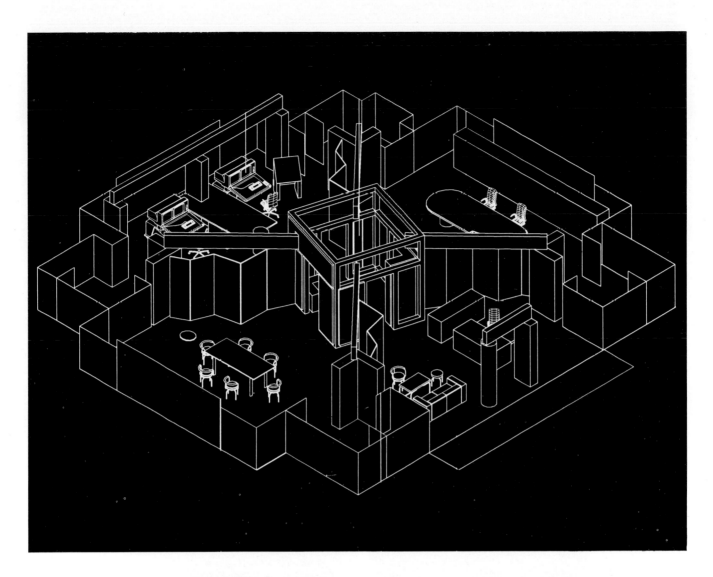

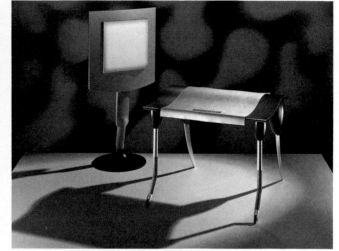

Silicon Valley; it promised to enhance the process of design and move it into the Space Age. With stereolithography apparatus, the design of an object can be transferred from the computer screen via laser beam directly into a liquid-filled processor that produces a "hard," transparent, miniature three-dimensional model in ten minutes. The technique eliminates costly hand- or factory-built prototype models that take much time and money to produce.

Demonstrating that the student generation of the 1980s was clearly going to revolutionize design in the 1990s, graduate students at the Cranbrook Academy of Art, under the direction of Katherine and Michael McCoy, co-chairs of the Industrial and Graphic Design Department, moved into the future, studying upcoming technologies such as fiber-optics and plasma screens and producing some prototypical office furniture. The work combined beauty with movement, a symbiotic combination that took a more sophisticated approach to high technology.

However, it was the world of rock music and entertainment that kept moving toward the outer envelope of spatial experience. Designing discos across the country, Robert Doornick experimented with digitized lighting programmed to pulsate and "dance" to the music—along with laser beams, moving floors, walls, ceilings, and furniture. One of his projects introduced a six-foot robot, arriving from an aperture in the ceiling as if from outer space. This mechanical personality was controlled to interact with people on the dance floor who seemed not to be having as much fun as others. The ultimate purpose was to engage everyone in the nightclub and make them feel "needed." Doornick, an engineer, psychologist, and self-taught philosopher, was dedicated to a goal of involving people with technology and convincing them of its exhilarating benefits. By designing unique, big-budget nightclubs, he was able to fund other socially useful programs such as robots for health care that look after the elderly and infirm, giving them a sense of independence that a human nurse cannot. (He even foresees robots as replacing the pet dog for socially responsive activity, fetching slippers or newspapers.) At present these mechanical wonders are controlled by means of infrared beams or magnetic strips in the flooring. A machine that actually functions like a human has yet to be developed, though programmers are working on this objective at MIT's Artificial Intelligence Laboratory, and in the nearby Media Laboratory. Already the Media Lab has developed phones that can chat and "talking heads" (disembodied faces of real people) that gesture and converse by projecting video images. These are so lifelike that users of the system have felt that they were "meeting" with people speaking from another city. With interplanetary civilization a possibility, the scientific mind continues to probe the unexplained. The gap between the measurable and the immeasurable narrows. In the words of the philosopher William Irwin Thompson: "Mystical perceptions that started out as heresy end up as heritage." As David Bowie sang, we are destined for the stars.

Opposite page: Into the future using fiber optic technologies and plasma screens: Students at Cranbrook Academy come up with some far-out furniture designs (*top and center*) while students at the University of Illinois design a prototypical office (*bottom*) for the postindustrial society.

CHAPTER 3

The walls come tumbling down at the Best Products showroom in Houston, done by SITE in 1975 as a sociological narrative on the state of urban decay.

Heard of a van that's loaded with
    weapons,
Packed up and ready to go.
Heard of some gravesites out by the
    highway,
A place where nobody knows.
The sound of gunfire off in the distance:
I'm getting used to it now.
But I lived in a brownstone, lived in a
    ghetto.
I've lived all over this town.
This ain't no party, this ain't no disco,
This ain't no fooling around.
No time for dancing or lovey dovey.
I ain't got time for that now.

THE JAGGERED EDGE

Along the highway on the outskirts of Houston, Texas, can be glimpsed what appears to be a bombed-out shell of a building. The jagged edges of the facade and the cascade of crumbling bricks suggest that urban rioting and looting have left their mark on this high-tech city of NASA and heart transplants. But as one drives closer to the scene, it becomes clear that this building is "for real." People are parking in front, going inside to shop, and wheeling their carts of merchandise back to their cars. Indeed, business has never been better at the Best Products showroom. When it was first opened in 1975, this architectural aberration put its creators, SITE (Sculpture in the Environment), a team of artists headed by James Wines and Alison Sky, on the world media stage. They had dramatized a typical "shoebox" building on a typical American suburban "strip" that ordinarily would be considered unworthy of serious architectural attention. But worse, in the eyes of those who saw design as a serious occupation, they had approached the task with dark humor. Rather as rock music stars such as the Talking Heads provide social commentary through music in the guise of "entertainment," Wines and Sky seemed to be summarizing the critical state of urban decay—the hopelessness and anarchy of ghetto living—while at the same time offering a "fun" place to shop for consumer goods. SITE's approach was completely different from that of Robert Venturi (see Chapter 1), who viewed "juxtapositions of honky-tonk elements" as "all right" in his manifesto, *Complexity and Contradiction in Architecture.* And it was quite contrary, also, to the Modern style, with its obsession for building in response to utopian formulas. SITE, by drawing from sociological and psychological sources in the contemporary world, was searching for a design position outside of traditional Modernism and decorative historicist Post-Modernism. They compared the concept to the storytelling characteristics of performance art, video art, dance, and figurative painting. Narrative architecture, they said, was a way of using buildings to reflect "the constantly unfolding drama of the contemporary environment."

But "legitimate" members of the design community refused to see the parallels SITE made between its work and fourteenth-century Italian churches or palaces and Gothic religious structures, with their highly communicative walls that "could be read as shape, form, and texture on a purely visual level and trenchant observation on a literary and psychological level." The mean-spirited establishment moved to discuss ways of enacting legislation to prevent firms like SITE from taking jobs away from "real" architects. Meanwhile, the owners of the Best Products enterprise were laughing all the way to the bank. The Indeterminate Facade, as the work was called, together with its 1972 predecessor in Richmond, Virginia, called the Peeling Project (because certain portions of the brick veneer were peeled away and extended precariously into space), were an enormous success in providing a public image

Opposite page: After Armageddon? SITE's showrooms for Best Products depict a crumbling world in Houston (*top*), Sacramento (*center*), Cutler Ridge (*bottom*), and Milwaukee (*opposite right*).

and increasing sales. So much so that the socially conscious artists at SITE were commissioned to create other stores with similarly controversial design themes. For Sacramento, California, came the 1977 "Notch" showroom, with a jagged cut in one corner; and for Towson, Maryland, there was the "Tilt" showroom, done in 1978, in which the facade was tilted up from the ground on one side. At Cutler Ridge, Miami, the facade was segmented into four pieces so that the fragments created a surrealistic landscape of disconnected structures. This was one of two showrooms built in 1979 in Miami. The other at Hialeah, called the "Water" showroom, was a living iconography of the surrounding environment, including water, a grove of palm trees, earth, and rocks. It was inspired by local resentment at the intrusion of commercial enterprise into the area. And the themes continued in Richmond, Virginia, with the "Forest" showroom, integrating a natural environment that would have been demolished in the usual way for such a "strip" structure. Then in 1984 came the Milwaukee, Wisconsin, "Inside/Outside" showroom, which employed a double facade. The first was a fragmented one of brick, and the second one of glass that revealed the normal hidden elements of structure (ducts, plumbing, and lathe) and created a ghostly, architectural skeleton. Merchandise in the windows was "frozen" in place with an all-over blanket of dusty gray paint. It looked as though the store had been ripped apart by looters. But the satirical aspect of this work was not lost on the design community—SITE was exposing material that, normally, the average architect would go to great lengths to hide!

Making a point. Christo wraps a million square feet of Australian coastline in fabric (*top*) to lure public attention back to nature. Graffiti artists express hostility to urban living on New York subways (*bottom*).

The establishment fought back with a by-invitation-only show extended to friends of Philip Johnson who were asked to present facades for Best Products showrooms at the Museum of Modern Art, New York, in a special exhibition in 1979. But none of those drawings and concepts had the vitality or drama represented in the urban storytelling design themes of SITE, or had the support of an actual client. Thus the official "salon" favorites suddenly woke up to find themselves the new *refusés*.

In presenting the story of a disintegrating cityscape, SITE's attitudes were in concert with other artistic happenings of the era. Graffiti by ghetto teenagers—written on subway cars and in other public places—while the bane of city government, was the subject of a best-selling book, *The Faith of Graffiti*, documented by Jon Naar and Mervin Kurlansky, with an essay by Norman Mailer. The authors believed that the spray-can decorations were folk art—a unique public art form. "Art has been saying with more and more intensity: the nature of the painting has become less interesting than the nature of the relation of painting to society," declared Mailer. Other art happenings of the time, such as those by Chris Burden (who did a "piece" called *Shoot* in which he got shot in the arm with a .22 rifle), and work by artists such as Christo, Dennis Oppenheim, and Robert Smithson, strongly supported this radical new way of seeing things.

California collisions. Frank Gehry's work reflects the disorderly Los Angeles landscape in its use of cheap industrial materials such as chain-link fencing, corrugated aluminum, and raw plywood. This page, his own house is shown inside and out. Opposite, the Norton beach house and the Aerospace Museum in Los Angeles.

73

In Los Angeles, architect Frank Gehry had been pursuing some "far out" ideas of his own since setting up practice in 1962. Through psychoanalysis, Gehry learned to channel his anger, pain, and fear of existing in a hostile world into a series of brilliant architectural statements. Using unexpected and confrontational basic raw materials (such as plywood, cardboard, chain-link fencing, and corrugated metal, which he had used as a GI assigned to constructing ad hoc buildings at Fort Benning, Georgia), he set about making houses that attracted attention by looking "unfinished," or arrested in the midst of an explosion, with portions of walls skewed at odd angles or balanced precariously on top of one another. For his own house, which he worked on in 1977, he literally encased a banal suburban box in a cocoon of chain-link fencing and corrugated metal and left unfinished plywood exposed in interior rooms. The brutal conglomerations of these raw and often gashed materials fit right into their location. With their crashed corners and odd joints, they refer to industrial sheds, parking lots, lumberyards, and buildings under construction—in short, all of the insubstantiality that's part of the disorderly L.A. landscape. In addition, southern California was still reacting to the 1960s "tune in, turn on, drop out" Haight-Ashbury syndrome, which had permeated the West Coast. The Frank Gehry houses expressed antiarchitecture, antiestablishment ideas; they seemed literally to be blowing the system apart. Gehry's designs gained considerable media attention and a clientele for whom living in a much-publicized home by a much-publicized architect didn't hurt. The Gehry style identified a new generation of artists, stars, and filmmakers who were on the cutting edge of show business, communications, and the art world.

Gehry even showed how a nontraditional material—corrugated cardboard—could be interpreted into furniture and create a whole new inspiration for rooms. It was a kind of West Coast smoke signal: cheap, throwaway materials or objects could have their place in the living room and bedroom. Milk crates, standard doors, leftover pieces of lumber and glass, thrift-shop finds, old quilts and textiles, industrial lights, old car seats, antiquated plumbing fixtures, bits of stained glass and ceramic tile—the more rough and unready, the better they expressed a desire to recycle and thus avoid consumerism and waste. There were more economical and responsible things in life to do than to save up to invest in a conventional three-piece bedroom suite. But Gehry, while inciting revolution, was not prepared to lead it. When his cardboard pieces were suddenly tagged "art" by dealers and clients—who were already assigning reverence to faithful copies of Campbell soup cans—and began to change hands at suitably upscale gallery prices, he withdrew them from the market because this ran counter to his ideological intention.

However, the influence of the socially conscious, disarrayed future was rippling outward. Those Hollywoodites who found Gehry's creations too hard-edged soon had the opportunity to employ other talents who delivered the "undesigned" or ad hoc style in their own individual ways. They included Gehry disciples Eric Moss, Frank Israel, Fred Fisher, Coy Howard, Craig Hodgetts, Robert Mangurian, and Thom Mayne. Later, there were William Adams and Brian Murphy, who delighted his clients by creating occasional tables from odd pieces of picket fencing or cardboard beer crates topped with old tablecloths.

At the Institute for Architecture and Urban Studies in New York, where the alternative design directions were being investigated throughout the period from 1970 to 1980 (see Chapter 1), Peter Eisenman, the director, and fellow architect Andrew Mac-Nair pursued "underground" personalities who were destined for future acknowledgement as pacemakers and whose counterattacks on Modernism were not limited to the pursuit of history and memory. The conceptual artist Gordon Matta-Clark was invited to exhibit in an "Idea as Model" show. He had studied architecture at Cornell but rejected the profession after graduation because of its conservatism, choosing instead to pursue a particularly idiosyncratic guerilla-like strategy that certainly drew attention to his displeasure with "legitimate" building. Armed with chain saw or rifle, he literally cut structures up and blew them apart. These were statements of anarchitecture, criticisms of the national culture responding, he said, to "the ever less viable state of privacy, private property and isolation." Matta-Clark was dismissed by most as a maverick (he died of cancer in 1978 at the age of thirty-five, and it was to be ten years before he was formally recognized with a retrospective exhibition at the Brooklyn Museum as a major cultural contributor); however, his ideas were not entirely out of kilter with what Eisenman in particular was entertaining on his drawing board. "The activity of architecture is part of the fabric of man's activity in general, and major dislocations, no matter what their origin, necessarily ripple through...," he observed. Eisenman was concerned with posing questions within the structure of houses about the nature of structure and jolting ordinary perceptions about design. It was narrative architecture with perhaps a narrower, more esoteric field of criticism, and some of his clients later lamented that they were not altogether pleased with the way Eisenman used his private commissions as a kind of laboratory for experimentations, especially when there were intentional gaps in the bedroom floor, so that one could not step out of bed easily. To Eisenman's way of thinking, however, his experimentations were pure poetry and evolved from a design code plucked from linguistic theory.

Understanding what Eisenman is trying to convey is not altogether easy and, indeed, it took him thirteen years to express it himself in *House of Cards,* a manifesto book finally published in 1987. The title gives a clue to his hand. Building houses of playing cards implies precarious balance, collapse, and disintegration—an architectural contradiction, because a building is intended to be secure and enduring. To Eisenman,

Opposite page:
West Coast expressions
of radical design from
Fred Fisher at the Caplin
residence (*top left*);
from William Adams at
Archilla store (*top right*);
from Eric Moss in the
Petal residence (*center*);
and from Brian Murphy
in a private residence
(*bottom*).

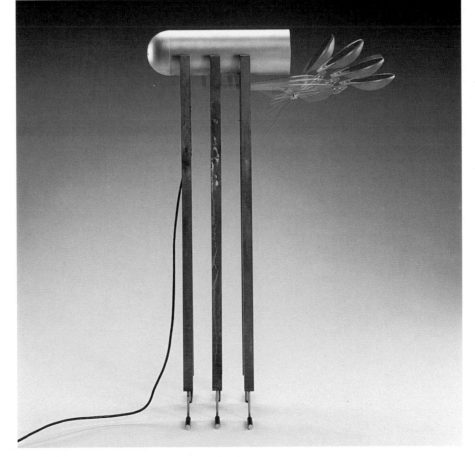

Thom Mayne and
Michael Rotundi
transform a bank into
the fashionable Kate
Mantelini's restaurant
(*top*) and offer a
barking-dog security lamp
(*bottom*) that responds to
the user's commands.

however, a building is itself a manifestation of dislocation, arising from humankind's exploration beyond the precinct of the cave. Recent design and building, he claims, have been created in the service of "institutions" perpetuating established conventions. Eisenman believes in disrupting these institutions—that is to say, for example, designing a dining room in which the conventions of dining are destroyed by placing a structural column beside the dining table, preventing an easy assembly of chairs or movement around the table, or building a stairway that goes to nowhere but a blank wall instead of accessing another level in the normal manner. He finds these statements symbolically appropriate in the post-Hiroshima world, in which "it is no longer certain that life will be marked by a stone or a cross, progeny or history. These once inviolate canons of death have now been rendered contingencies of an uncertain future. These uncertainties call into question the symbolism of all such markers of identity, not just those ultimate ones but the daily institutions of church, school, house." The Eisenman-designed house does not allude to creature comfort, which he believes to be meaningless, but is more concerned with dispensing shock value and an overall sense of anxiety, which may be achieved through the use of transparent glass walls inside, and opaque concrete windowless walls on the outside, or by putting up a nonsupporting column (the latter is more of a shock to an architect than anyone else).

Since 1970, when he was chosen for inclusion in a book called *Five Architects* (Eisenman, Michael Graves, Charles Gwathmey, John Hejduk, Richard Meier), Eisenman has been influenced by Hejduk, the unconventional dean of architecture at Cooper Union, who asks students to design a building in the spirit of a Mondrian painting or the style of a Proust novel and through such deconstruction and examination of another art form attempt to give design a connectedness. Reaching toward other artistic disciplines, Eisenman was led to the work of the European philosophers Ferdinand de Saussure, Michel Foucault, and, particularly, Jacques Derrida, who invented the "Deconstruction" theory of literary criticism. Briefly explained, Deconstructionism is about undermining oppositions. The concept is to attack generally accepted dualistic assumptions, such as "Truth is more important than fiction," and to show that neither is more important than the other—that both coexist equally. Translated into design by Eisenman, the effort is to make architecture more "real" by reason of the fictional or storytelling content that is put into it. With this rendition of Derridian theory into design and architecture, Eisenman hit on an intellectual premise for explaining mavericks such as the SITE people and Matta-Clark. It stimulated other designers to investigate dislocation and anarchic collapse and to comment on the imperfections of American culture.

In 1982, Chicago-based Stanley Tigerman produced a book called *Versus, An American Architect's Alternatives*, calling for architects to "represent at once the sacred and the profane."

Works by Gordon Matta-Clark—*Splitting* (top and center), done in 1974, and *Window Blowout* (bottom), executed in 1976—draw attention to the inadequacy of "legitimate" buildings.

Disruptions in House VI by Peter Eisenman include a column that gets in the way of the dining table and an awkward slit in the living-room ceiling.

Opposite page: Stanley Tigerman's attempts to produce architectural dislocation result in the phallus-shaped Daisy house (*top*), the Anti-Cruelty Society (*center*) with its friendly-canine facade, and the corrugated metal weekend cottage (*bottom*), all of which combine the sacred and the profane.

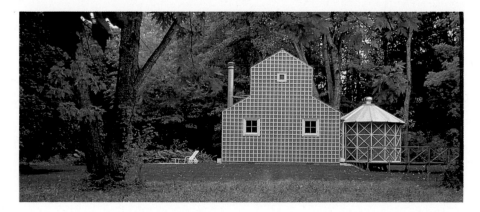

This was evidenced in his work at the Daisy House, designed in the imprint of a phallus, in which the sacred shelter or "home" was invaded with a theme of sex; the Hot Dog House, cast in the shape of a sausage and evoking middle-American eating habits; and the Bagel House, intended for a "Jewish American princess." For the Anti-Cruelty Society in Chicago (where unadopted animals are destroyed), Tigerman built a metaphorical facade of a friendly dog. For his own modest weekend place on Lake Michigan, he fashioned corrugated metal into a circular "baptistry"—screened-in porch cum dining room—attached to a barnlike "cathedral" structure. The house is approached from a wicket gate that opens onto a curving wooden walkway. Located in a small, conservative neighborhood, the "cottage" caused havoc every weekend on the quiet tree-lined streets, attracting dozens of rubbernecking drivers intent on getting a glimpse of the "far out" design. The town fathers were appalled and promptly forbade further building in corrugated metal.

Rubberneckers also lined up in New York during a 1984 event called Designer's Saturday to view the Modern Mode showroom by Paul Haigh. The queue was so long that it took two hours to get into the space. Haigh—an all-round designer known for his furniture, interiors, and architecture—was involved in what he called Post-Industrial design, literally turning all the codes of Modernism on edge. Introducing a series of cubes within the 3,000-square-foot space, he lifted them up on spheres, pyramids, and cones so that they appeared to be toppling over on these bizarre supports. It was his personal semaphore for the dislocation of Modernism, the pure forms of the circle, triangle, and square being violated by warped intervention. But it was also a cue for other younger-generation designers intent on saying that they were beyond Modernism but not part of the Post-Modern camp. Tilting walls, off-center furniture legs, and rough-cut edges became part of what was defined in a book by Robert Janjigian as *High Touch, the New Materialism.* Andrew Batey and Mark Mack, a team in San Francisco, brought concrete blocks into the bedroom, using them for walls, seating, and a bed. Samuel de Santo, a New York architect and professor at the New York Institute of Technology, daringly introduced them in the Manhattan showroom of Steelcase, a leading office furniture company, putting this conservative firm up several notches in terms of design image.

Particularly successful at juxtaposing raw materials was New Yorker Kevin Walz, a painter and sculptor who turned to interior and furniture design in the mid-1980s. He was very inventive, putting a high-tech metal bed against raw timber plank walls or rich silk against a rough-textured metal table and other pieces of furniture made of concrete. The East Coasters had a way of making the West Coasters' head-on-collision style more palatable and glamorous for more conservative, traditionally minded clients.

In 1985, with the fortieth anniversary of the end of World War II, international attention refocused on the destruction of Europe and Japan, reminding people that current nuclear technology could now destroy the planet. At the same time, survivors of World War II concentration camps (guided by inspiration from the awesome black granite Vietnam memorial in Washington) were persuaded to recall their suppressed grief and anger and share with future generations the memory of the Holocaust through tangible structures. A standard bearer was writer and Holocaust survivor Elie Wiesel, given world recognition with the Nobel Peace Prize in 1986 as well as with a Distinguished American Congressional Medal of Honor from President Reagan at the one-hundredth anniversary celebration of the Statue of Liberty. Large-scale fund-raising campaigns were inaugurated in the Jewish communities of New York, Washington, and Miami to build Holocaust memorials that would leave an archeological imprint on those cities.

But in addition to the fear of nuclear annihilation—perhaps due to the recklessness of some politician pushing the red button—there was a renewed recognition of the threat of pollution, both radioactive and otherwise. This arose partly because of the 1979 mishap at Three Mile Island nuclear plant and the 1986 accident at the Soviet Union's Chernobyl nuclear plant,

Monument to 57,661 killed and 2,500 unaccounted for, the somber black granite Vietnam Veterans' Memorial by Maya Ying Lin points to the futility of war and the fragility of life on this earth.

the radioactive fallout from which affected countries thousands of miles away. These events emphasized the fragility of life on the planet even without actual military combat. Acid rain from air pollution and the greenhouse effect, caused by the excessive buildup of fluorocarbons in the atmosphere (from automobile exhausts and all those spray cans of hair gunk), groundwater pollution from chemical fertilizers and pesticides (the green-lawn and shiny-red-apple syndromes)—all these were signs of a severely threatened environment.

Unconsciously or consciously, some designers reacted to record the crumbling of society. Small boutiques that appealed to a hip, punk generation—well-versed in the music of the Talking Heads, Pink Floyd, The Clash, The Sex Pistols, and Midnight Oil—were built in concrete, with a stark bunker-like quality. New restaurants, bars, and clubs, like Manhattan's Tunnel, that looked as if they had somehow survived a nuclear Armageddon, began to appear. In San Francisco, a small firm called Ace Architects worked on small stores with fractured, toppling facades. Graphic designers like Michael Vanderbyl in San Francisco were fast becoming tuned into the new mood, coming up with jagged-edged stationery and cutout features in their print work that alluded to the propensity for disintegration.

The New York firm of Hardy Holzman Pfeiffer—who had achieved notoriety for their "subversive" rebuilding of a New York brownstone in which members of the radical Weathermen group had been blown up in the mid-1960s (this may have been one of the earliest models of design dislocation)—did a renovation of Brooklyn's famous 1903 Majestic Theater. Although this structure had been in a state of decay for thirty years, the architects made few changes in it, allowing raw brick and aging paintwork to remain untouched, so the audience would be shoulder to shoulder with the effects of disrepair and the ravages of time. Because some intervention was necessary to "create" this ruin, critics attacked the concept, warning that the effect would be fleeting, while others argued that this calculated dissolution was better than a modern "sanitization" and more appropriate for the borough of Brooklyn. "It is literally a decadent building," wrote critic Michael Kimmelman in *The New York Times,* "a place where crumbling plaster, broken column capitals, and cracked archways have been carefully preserved, and in more than a few cases, artfully stage-managed."

In its new Bayard Building headquarters on Bleecker Street, SITE—whose leader, James Wines, was the newly appointed chairman of the Environmental Design Department at New York's Parsons School of Design, following a critical reevaluation of the schools' curriculum—found another original way of expressing disintegration. In the Bayard Building, completed in 1898 and the only example of Louis Sullivan's architecture in New York City, SITE treated the only loft space, with its original decorative details, to a careful renovation for its ever-growing team of artists and designers. Stationary walls with metal egg-and-dart cornices and wood bases were constructed of wire lathe over exposed metal studs. This design suggested the narrative of the industrial building, and the partial walls evoked the ghosts of the past.

For Willi Smith, a sportswear fashion star on New York's Seventh Avenue, SITE came up with an urban-ghetto street scene with sidewalk, fire hydrants, chain-link fence, and fire escapes all painted a brutal gray, against which models in WilliWear's tough street clothes paraded, to create a sense of "reality." The design won an *Interiors* Award in 1985 and proved to mark the beginning of SITE's acceptance by the elite architectural and design community. On the jury was James Stewart Polshek, then dean of the Columbia University School of Architecture, who praised the work for reflecting "sociopolitical" attitudes of "disintegration." (He may have had an axe to grind as co-founder of the antinuclear Architects, Designers, and Planners for Social Responsibility.) But his equally enthusiastic co-jurors, Hugh Newell Jacobsen, Neville Lewis, and Natalie de Blois, represented mainstream design thinking. Meanwhile SITE continued to push on to the outer edges of the envelope, producing a "new" precrushed plastic bottle for Vittel water.

Toppling facades (*top*) in the Gnome Sweet Gnome and Country stores by Ace Architects in San Francisco speak to urban and sociological disintegration. The interiors of the Max Protech New York gallery (*bottom*) are deliberately unfinished.

Urban ghetto streetscape (top) by SITE for WilliWear emphasizes the tough nature of youthful contemporary street clothes. The Tunnel Club (bottom), designed by Peter Michael Marino, reuses a raw, underground-railroad environment.

In the ruined 1903 Majestic Theater in Brooklyn, Hardy Holzmann Pfeiffer preserved and sometimes stage-managed decadence.

But most telling in terms of the influence of this new design tendency was the appointment of Bernard Tschumi as dean of the School of Architecture, Planning and Preservation at Columbia University, to succeed James Stewart Polshek, in 1987. Tschumi had just completed a series of pavilions or "follies" at the Parc de la Villette in Paris, which spoke to his concept of fragmentation in design. He illustrates this in his lectures by showing a slide of an exploding star and drawing parallels between what has been made by humanity and by God.

Fractal by Benoit B. Mandelbrot, demonstrates unpredictable irregularity in natural phenomena.

This reference to astronomy, physics, and entropy relates to the science of chaos, which, since the 1970s, has been cutting across traditional academic thought. In studying realities once considered rigid, physicists and mathematicians, using computers and special kinds of graphic images, have discovered that the universe may be based upon disorder rather than rationality. They have captured a fantastic structure underlying the complexity of life. This new science has created its own new language—the "butterfly effect," "fractals," "attractors," and "folded-towel diffeomorphisms." Inherent order is being discovered in disorder. In other words, patterns that make sense can be defined within chaos, and these have their own geometry. Within the asymmetry and seeming nonlinear randomness of nature there are constant, repetitive themes. For many thinkers even outside the world of physics, chaos has become a science of process—a state of becoming rather than one of being. These revelations have been documented in numerous publications, especially in James Gleick's valuable book *Chaos*, published in 1987.

Given all this input, it was clearly time in 1988 for a grand statement to be made with a design exhibition. The idea of a show titled "Violated Perfection" originated in Chicago at the suggestion of Paul Florian and Stephen Wierzbowski, at the University of Illinois, but funds failed to materialize. Aaron Betsky, a Gehry disciple, passed the idea along to Philip Johnson, at age eighty-two still an active member of the board of trustees of New York's Museum of Modern Art. And thus emerged, at MoMA in July 1988, "Deconstructivist Architecture," a show of the work of seven architects: Frank Gehry, Daniel Libeskind (former head of architecture at the Cranbrook Academy), Peter Eisenman, and Bernard Tschumi representing the United States and Zaha Hadid, an Iranian-born designer based in London, Rem Koolhaas, from Amsterdam, and the Viennese team of Coop Himmelblau (literally "blue sky"), making up the rest.

Not surprising was the uproar that followed the selection. Questions centered on who was in, who was not in, and why. Notably absent was the firm of SITE, whose worldwide reputation as protagonists of Deconstruction, now given its inevitable pop title "Decon," was surely irrefutable. They had a total of fifty-five works to their credit, and their scholarly manifesto *De-architecture* had just been published in Spring 1988 by

Rizzoli, establishing the theory they had been practicing for over twenty years. It turned out that the academics now distinguished two different species of Decon: Deconstruction and Deconstructivist. Princeton professor Mark Wigley, associate curator for the MoMA show, defined the chosen ones as Deconstructives because they did not dismantle buildings, but located "inherent dilemmas within buildings. The Deconstructive architect puts the pure forms of the architectural tradition on the couch and identifies the symptoms of a repressed impurity. The impurity is drawn to the surface by a combination of gentle coaxing and violent torture: the form is interrogated."

In so doing, he went on to explain, the Deconstructivists developed their strategies from the early-twentieth-century Soviet avant garde known as Russian Constructivists, who posed "threats to tradition" and produced "impure," skewed, geometric compositions as a way of noting that they belonged to the new industrialized-aeronautical-political-revolutionary era. These artists, led by Kazimir Malevich, produced drawings and models of radical structures that "bent" tradition to open up "disturbing architectural possibilities" via warped planes, diagonal overlapping, shattered grids, and other disquieting images.

Portrait of I.V. Kliun by Russian Constructivist Kazimir Malevich.

These forms never got built, but the drawings and art works remain to explain their unsettling visions. According to Wigley, however, the Constructivists' projects represent a totally different idea from the work of Deconstructionists such as SITE, Eric Moss, Morphosis, and Hardy Holzman Pfeiffer, whose efforts are engaged in a rather more potent physical dislocation of structures. Yet the purpose of Deconstruction is to alter perception, according to SITE's James Wines, and thereby a connection to the Deconstructivist is evident.

Whether the designer is a Deconstructivist or a Deconstructionist, however, will matter little in terms of design history. Both will be known for following the Decon idiom. And in all probability, history will see the Decon record as a manifestation of a turbulent time in our society, when wars, armaments, acts of terrorism, and ecological disasters were daily topics and inner cities were uneasy, disruptive neighborhoods where dope was peddled, crime was rampant, and life was tenuous. In Norman Mailer's words: "We are at the possible end of civilization, and our instinct, battered, all polluted, dreams of some cleansing we have not found...."

Nevertheless, as the 1990s get under way, more optimistic signs are emerging as a result of warnings from the arts, design, and environmentally minded constituencies. A realignment away from disaster is a conceivable possibility, with energy provided at the grass-roots level to change the ponderous course of government and bureaucracies. Decentralization, regionalism, and the think-global–act-local slogan of the indefatigable environmentalists are the current measures of redemption.

CHAPTER 4

Building for people by people. Indian cliff dwellings at Mesa Verde.

Imagine no possessions,

I wonder if you can

No need for greed or hunger:

A brotherhood of man.

Imagine all the people

Sharing all the world,

You may say I'm a dreamer

But I'm not the only one

I hope some day you'll join us

And the world will be as one.

In 1970, design students were drawn to a cluster of hand-built, ad hoc buildings in the Arizona desert just north of Phoenix to hear the words of a master who taught a new discipline called Arcology while selling handmade bells to cover his living expenses. Soon the master began to receive national and international attention from cultural institutions. Museums were interested in exhibiting the master's drawings, and publications sought photographs of the campus. Curators wanted to know more about his philosophy. The master's name was Paolo Soleri and he was a charismatic figure, most often giving lectures in shorts and singlet. He drew plans of cities in which people lived, worked, and played in megatowers, commuting from one activity to the other by banks of escalators. Much of the energy required for these great buildings was to be generated by the sun, which Soleri believed was a vastly underutilized source of natural economic power. His concepts included an appealing way of life in which the air- and noise-polluting car was made obsolescent for daily transportation and the natural environment—trees, green parks, rolling hills—was to be used by all for pleasure and enjoyment and to be found but a stone's throw from the self-supporting minicity. This building type illustrated the concept of Arcology, a synthesis of architecture and ecology, which Soleri had developed in the 1940s as he studied at nearby Taliesen West with Frank Lloyd Wright, learning about organic design that fitted into the natural landscape.

Student "workshoppers" who joined the Soleri campus soon learned that the path to utopia can be arduous and rough. With restricted funds, mostly from private donors, experimental building went on with minimal sophistication. Often students were forced to make their own nails or to hand-carry concrete, because there was little building equipment and no other resources were available. But these stumbling blocks did not outweigh the principles they learned: to build in harmony with sun, wind, and earth; to use nature as a resource that had boundless beneficence. They found out that standard air-conditioning was not essential for creature comfort, even in the broiling 100-degree-plus desert. By building underground, it was possible to maintain an even 56 degrees in an interior space. And underground shelters did not have to be cavelike, gloomy, uninviting, or confining. They could have imaginatively placed small skylights, and be constructed in marvelous organic shapes, in whitewashed stucco. They learned how to use the sun's shade and shadow and how to create wind tunnels in aboveground structures so that workshops could be cool and refreshing places. The knowledge gained in the hands-on experience with Soleri was uplifting and exhilarating, not just because of its application to design and building but for its farsighted solutions to basic organizational problems. Soleri said: "We cannot continue just providing people with shelter and nothing else, we have to shelter social systems. If you structure the shelter for society, then individuals will find their place.

A proposed urban arcology by Paolo Soleri.

Designing in harmony
with natural elements,
sun, shade, and wind,
Paolo Soleri creates a
new design code.

Fire employed by a suburban homesteader (*top*) and a city homeless person (*bottom*).

We have to design culturally rich cities, not just bedroom suburbs. Land and manufacturing are essential because we must be self-supporting, we cannot be parasitic, every community needs the arts and performances; otherwise they're just survival machines."

At a time when urban infrastructure, mass transportation systems, affordable housing, and quality public educational systems seemed to be falling apart and suburban charms had been at least partially destroyed by a realization that bucolic isolation does not inevitably provide contentment, Soleri's consciouness-raising to larger issues was invigorating. It was true that in actuality he was demonstrating his beliefs on a small scale, due to limited finances; but nevertheless there was a guiding light to a more hopeful future, which has been maintained ever since.

It took an architect tied into the established system to turn the essence of the Soleri concept into reality. Atlanta's John Portman saw an opportunity in the failing inner cities for a new kind of people-oriented environment that would draw citizens back to enjoy an exhilarating urban existence. His first attempt, completed in 1976 in his native Atlanta, was the Peachtree Center in the heart of downtown. A complex of tall, shimmering, glass megabuildings, it was designed to offer a multitude of activities and meeting places. It combined a 1,074-room 73-story hotel, shopping mall, conference center, bars, clubs, restaurants, and office space. The heart of the structure was a glass-skylighted multistory atrium, landscaped with trees and waterfalls and offering space for overscale art works. Glass-enclosed elevators, visible from the atrium and decorated with circus-like lighting, move up and down, contributing to the twinkling, kaleidoscopic atmosphere. The structure was not solar-powered, as Soleri had intended; indeed, it was a gargantuan consumer of energy via standard heating and cooling, but the concept of multiple uses for easy access and convenience was certainly there. "What I wanted to do," Portman explained, "was to create buildings and environments that really are for people, not a particular class of people but all people."

Just as developers and governments dismissed Soleri for his unrealistic ideas, tunnel-vision people found fault with the Portman premise. It was labeled a "plastic environment" that, like a great, isolated fortress, turned its back on the city and encouraged people not to go out on the streets. Portman countered: "I've been criticized for building great interior spaces— it's beyond belief. A city is a great and glorious thing. A city can stand great interior spaces as well as great exterior spaces. It's an orchestration of all kinds of environments that adds variety and interest and excitement to a city." In all events, Portman had hit on a magic formula that people liked and responded to, and it captured the attention of hotel operators who were reacting to a new travel idiom, the convention business. Lively downtown hotels could lure thousands to conventions and thus to the city, bringing business fallout and benefit all over downtown. Portman's concept worked. And it was reiterated in major metropolitan centers all over the country—the Embarcadero Plaza in San Francisco, Place Bonaventure in Los Angeles, Renaissance Center in Detroit, and others. (In an unusual professional departure, Portman took on the role of the architect-developer, in partnership with other financial backers and with overall control of construction, and was thus compensated financially far beyond the usual fees for his work.) As the buildings went up, still more criticisms erupted. The architectural tricks—atrium, glass-enclosed elevator pods, illuminated waterfalls, art-work banners, cantilevered balconies—used in city after city gave a sense of déjà vu. The whole effect was "kitsch." In answer, Portman replied that the great interior space was meant "to lift the human spirit, an atrium is an example of positive effect on people." Official recognition eventually arrived. In 1978, to acknowledge his architectural contributions, Portman was awarded an American Institute of Architects medal for innovations in hotel design.

Portman's pursuit of the people and their tastes was perhaps instinctual—he felt it was necessary to entertain and to uplift, and then proceeded to weave into his designs glitter and glamour, flags and banners, sparkling water and marble flooring. This was his way of speaking to the need for an alternative design philosophy in the 1970s, when Charles Moore, Robert Venturi, Michael Graves, and Robert Stern were evolving the historicist contextual language (see Chapter 1); Peter Eisenman, Stanley Tigerman, and James Wines were using a narrative vocabulary to give architecture more meaning (see Chapter 2); and Joseph D'Urso, Helmut Jahn, and Michael Kalil were in search of a technological advance on Modernism (see Chapter 3). But this investigative strategy as to what people really wanted was already very much in the minds of some other thoughtful trailblazers, headed by David Lewis, former professor of Architecture and Urban Design at Carnegie Mellon University, an architect and planner based in Pittsburgh. He pointed out that up to this time buildings were designed for clients and only secondarily for the context in which they were sited. This was a sad mistake. Everyone was well aware of the loss of faith in urban planning, which had resulted in old neighborhoods being torn down for "urban renewal" and decimation of regional and local character. They understood that the bureaucratization and centralization of human habitats, as exemplified by the Pruitt-Igoe high-rise housing that had to be razed to the ground because of its unpopularity (see Chapter 1), had to be replaced by a more comfortable form of urban revitalization. Lewis declared: "In every city we have swept away old districts with a total disregard for the intricacy of sociocultural traditions, the ways of life and aspirations of the people in them, and we have replaced them with imposed conceptions of what the people should have. Glass-encased office blocks soar in disregard for the precise heritages of the streets on which they are built. Schools are built without windows,

Designing with people in mind, John Portman creates gargantuan complexes (*opposite*) not only for multiple uses but also to lift the spirit.

Bombed-out building in the blitzed city.

boxes in which an artificial mini-world called education is purveyed to children with scant recognition of the environmental resources and local traditions of the communities in which they are growing."

As a result of this clearly poor city planning, Regional/Urban Design Assistance Teams (or R/UDATs) were established by the American Institute of Architects for the express purpose of lending a hand to communities with planning problems and helping them find solutions through citizen participation. The service was instituted to deal with what was considered a deep undercurrent of public protest against the kind of centralization and secrecy of decision making that affects the lives and traditions of whole communities. It was intended to counteract the rising tide of protest against big business, shrewd developers, unintelligent and ruthless government—a sentiment best symbolized by the outcry over the Watergate political scandal and the subsequent resignation of President Nixon. Rarely were the citizens who lived in inner-city communities asked by the official designers of a project what their perceptions or goals were. Lewis, a prime mover in initiating the R/UDAT process, said the thought that the inhabitants might have different values and priorities from those of the planners, architects, and government agencies simply had not occurred to anyone! It was clearly time to remedy the situation.

Between 1967 and 1987, over eighty public investigations were accomplished. A typical R/UDAT team is never foisted on any community; it is invited. A group of about eight professionals from all over the country come to the site. These professionals are taken from different disciplines—architecture, town planning, sociology, law, landscape architecture, economics—and are all leaders in their fields. To ensure objectivity, they volunteer their time. Only their expenses are reimbursed. They are joined by an equal number of students from the nearby schools of architecture, urban design, and planning. The visit usually takes place over four days, beginning with a physical inspection of the study areas on foot as well as by bus, boat, or helicopter. Conferences are organized with city, business, and community leaders. On the second day, there is a town meeting, the first of two. Open to all interested citizens, its purpose is to collect input from individuals and nonestablishment groups. Then each member of the team works at his or her specialty, alone or in small groups—conceptualizing, writing, drawing, and conferring to compare thoughts and ideas.

Over the next forty-eight hours a plan is fleshed out and, by dawn of the fourth day, a finished book, usually sixty to one hundred pages in length, goes to the printer. In the afternoon there is a press conference and in the evening the second open town meeting. Here the team makes its presentation to the community, using slides and the finished report (miraculously back from the printer just in the nick of time) to illustrate its recommendations. In the twenty years of the program's operation, visits have ranged from investigations in small hamlets to

The Regional Urban
Design Assistance Teams
meet to help local
communities solve their
design problems.

others in major cities such as Birmingham, Alabama, and Denver, Colorado. Subjects have included problems that are generic in most urban and suburban communities: affordable housing (R/UDAT groups generally recommend rehabilitation of existing structures rather than rehousing in new building), revitalization of inner downtowns, reuse of railroad yards and terminal buildings, preservation of historical sites, conservation of green space in the face of rapid ongoing development, and maintenance of a shaky urban infrastructure (fire, sewer, police, transportation services) as a result of persistently inadequate funds.

A new terminology, called Process Architecture, developed as a result of these investigations, and it was used effectively by design practitioners who took the trouble to find out more about it. Charles Moore and William Turnbull, working on a commission from the University of California, used Process Architecture in the design of the 525-student Kresge College at Santa Cruz, completed in 1974. Both student groups and university officials were tapped as a committee of users. One of the committee's recommendations was to organize the residential areas as small clusters, to be known as "kin groups." These groups would operate as substitute families. This became an important recommendation, as it gave the architects an opportunity to design an environment that was less institutional and had more variety and human scale than is usual in residential colleges. In their design of the college, Moore and Turnbull employed the metaphor of a village, planning around the street "an open-air corridor that responds organically to the various activities that take place in the buildings along its route." The main lecture hall was treated as a town hall; the library was given an important portal; the laundry, symbolic of the village watering hole, was designed with a rather large triumphal arch. Everywhere the street was overlooked by balconies and terraces within the flanking buildings, so that the interrelationship between street and building, inside and outside, public and private, achieved at once an exciting intricacy and a unity.

The architects worked with students on furnishing their dormitories. Together they selected a Finnish plastic cube system. Each student was given what amounted to his or her own building block set (sixteen cubes), a desktop, a bedboard, a foam mattress, and a director's chair. From these elements, individual arrangements could be set up. Similar dialogues shaped the interior furnishings of the classrooms and common rooms. And colors were everywhere—red, yellow, bright green. Color was used to detail exterior facades. Intricate Mediterranean-style paving was employed to delineate the plazas along the street. Turnbull noted that when, after the completion of construction, an unforeseen problem occurred, the students took charge. "Because of their participatory activities, they had a feeling the place is theirs, to install their own alterations and additions and to resolve offending situations."

Charles Moore, who was to become the most highly paid architectural academician in the country when he took over as

Kresge College campus at Santa Cruz (*below and opposite page*), designed by Charles Moore and William Turnbull, creates a village environment in which the laundry (*bottom*) is given the prominence of the village well and students are given foam blocks with which to build their own personalized interiors.

the O'Neill Ford Professor of architecture at the University of Texas at Austin in 1987, strongly believed in Process Architecture and continued to use it in his public commissions throughout the 1970s and 1980s. In partnership with William Grover and Robert Harper in 1976, he took on a request to handle the development concept of 4½ miles of riverfront in Dayton, Ohio. Chadwick Floyd, a project director on the planning team, was responsible for organizing citizen participation. The goal was to make every person living within Dayton feel that he or she had a stake in the outcome. After several months of public-opinion polling from a shop front and on the streets, and also as well as working with local community groups, only 2,000 citizens had given input in a city of nearly one million people. There seemed only one way to reach the masses: television. In a unique experience, six one-hour-long television programs, called "Designathons," were mounted to capture "live" on-the-air viewer responses by telephone. The idea worked. As the viewers called in, they could see their ideas sketched on the spot; design and popular opinion met head-on in healthy discussion. The real value of Process Architecture, reported Moore and his team at the completion of the River Design Dayton task, was that a citywide sense of proprietorship emerged, an involvement and commitment that encouraged city government to get the job done.

Urban murals in San Francisco and Chicago bring color to city walls.

It was from these tentative experiments that enthusiastic citizen involvement spread from city to city. Suddenly blank walls were treated to colorful murals by local artists and abandoned lots became vegetable and flower gardens. And it was not always professional painters who did the work. Mural painting became popular art and scores of ordinary citizens became involved in giving their cityscape populist messages—of peace, ethnic pride, inner-urban renaissance. They were uplifting statements. Preservation and pride became tools for a new American civic revitalization.

In cities that had been torn apart by racial discord, as in Pontiac, Michigan, local citizen groups representing all ethnic communities got together to start planning community centers. In that city, architects David Lewis and Raymond Lindroz used the Process Architecture method to work out a complex problem that resulted in a building with learning areas for children and adults, a health center, theaters and a library, a community fieldhouse, offices for social services, a food co-op, workshops and studios, food services for the elderly, and a public restaurant and lounge. The designers described the "organic" nature of the process when people get to be involved in a hands-on situation. Most contemporary architects, they noted, appreciated the organic quality and visual richness of a Mediterranean or African town or village or the streets of European Renaissance cities without fully grasping that the human, hands-on element contributed to the success of these environments! Personal relationships with courtyards, footpaths, streets, steps, rainwater conduits, and portals built by

River Dayton Task Force helps citizens to decide on plans for the riverside through community outreach and live on-the-air television programs.

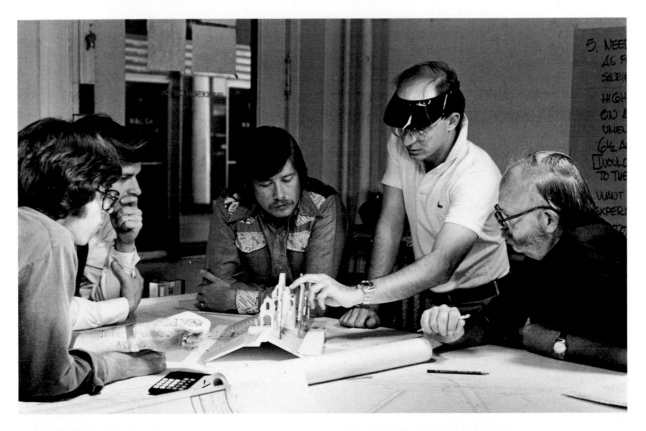

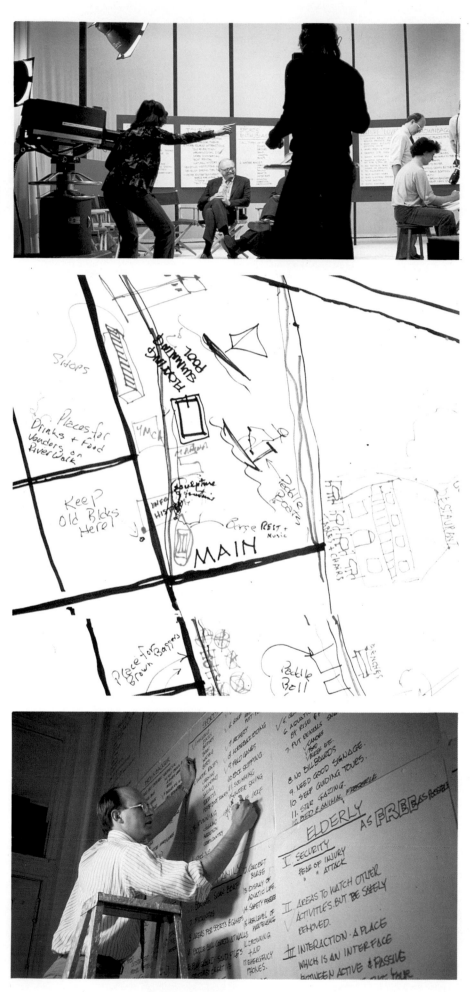

River Dayton design efforts produce a final plan that citizens feel is theirs.

109

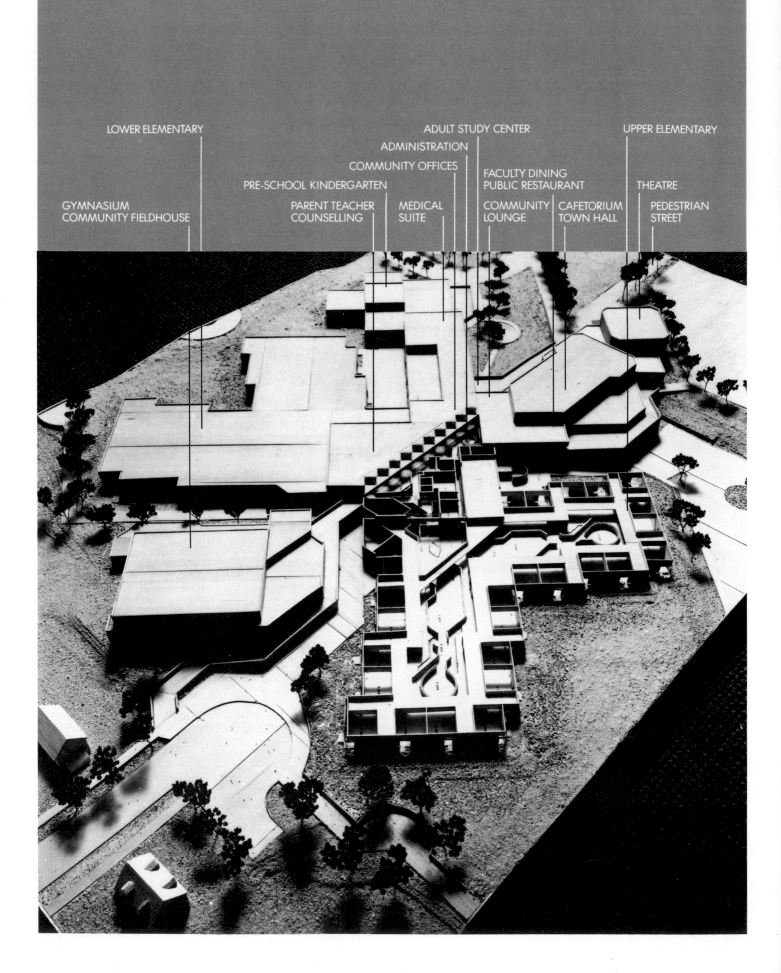

LOWER ELEMENTARY

ADULT STUDY CENTER

UPPER ELEMENTARY

ADMINISTRATION

COMMUNITY OFFICES

PRE-SCHOOL KINDERGARTEN

FACULTY DINING
PUBLIC RESTAURANT

THEATRE

GYMNASIUM
COMMUNITY FIELDHOUSE

PARENT TEACHER
COUNSELLING

MEDICAL
SUITE

COMMUNITY
LOUNGE

CAFETORIUM
TOWN HALL

PEDESTRIAN
STREET

the people themselves gave the location a friendly neighborhood feeling. By contrast, twentieth-century building done with powerful technology could dominate any scene, and it was often imposed by architects and designers living miles away from the site, with no relationship to the area at all. David Lewis and his partners worked on all sizes of projects using Process Architecture and design, including a major city-center, multi-use project in downtown Pittsburgh.

One example of a city that went defiantly on a new path directed by citizen input was Davis, California. In the early 1970s, faced with the prospect of an increase in population from 30,000 to 90,000 by 1990, a group of concerned citizens was formed. Called the Greater Davis Research Group, its purpose was to try to ward off this disquieting future. This group won a majority in a city council election in 1972, which indicated a concern for environmental issues over development-oriented interests. From there, Davis concentrated on examining how its citizens would live for the next twenty years. Research showed that energy consumption could be reduced by half, and thus citizens could benefit by stable living costs. Since 1974, a passive-solar energy-conservation building code has mandated a southerly orientation and light-colored walls and roofs, imposed standards for insulation, and restricted exterior glazing, giving credits for various kinds of shading and screening. And energy conservation has not been limited to building codes. Bike lanes were introduced and two wheels were favored over four as a means of transportation in order to reduce paving and to make the neighborhoods more pleasant. (Davis today counts two bicycles per adult.) To write these policies and implement these strategies, funding was acquired from the local university, the city, and the Department of Housing and Urban Development. In short, Davis proved to be a textbook example of grass-roots effort by the people for the people to achieve a healthier, more livable environment.

Late in the 1970s, one exceptionally perceptive developer took all this information into consideration, and focused on Boston. That city had been subjected to disastrous urban renewal in the 1960s. The civic buildings that the public most strongly disliked were austere and cold, offering no lively public spaces for enjoyment after work. The so-called renewal literally made people want to escape from downtown, when the plan had been just the opposite! James Rouse, based in Columbia, Maryland, had an idea for drawing people back to the downtown, bringing them to a neighborhood of historic charm and authenticity around the old seaport. The city's Faneuil Hall Market Place, built in 1742, had been standing empty for years alongside its companion buildings, the Quincy Market, added in 1823. The complex occupied six acres. Rouse produced an ambitious plan to rehabilitate these structures, bringing them back to their original glory and using them as linchpins for an indoor-outdoor shopping mall. With approval from the city and input from Benjamin Thompson, an imaginative local architect,

A multiple-use center in Pontiac, Michigan, by David Lewis of Urban Design Associates. Planned with hands-on participation from the community, this center helps to cement civic pride and ethnic diversity.

Opposite page:
Shopping as theater and
entertainment brings a
new concept to
downtown. Rouse
developments by
Benjamin Thompson at
South Street Seaport,
New York (*top*), Faneuil
Hall, Boston (*center*), and
Harbor Place, Baltimore
(*bottom*), also invigorate
historic landmarks.

Urbanism at its best in
the Marketplace at
Citicorp, New York, by
Hugh Stubbins.

Rouse proceeded to give Boston what was to become a model people-oriented place—a meeting ground for department stores, restaurants, casual stand-up snack bars, and various forms of street entertainment. No expense was spared. The budget was almost $20 million, and the quality of the rehabilitation—the attention to details such as street lighting, paving, signage, and art work—all combined to create a delightful public space. Soon over one hundred and fifty shops and restaurants were doing business in the 400,000 square feet of rentable space. It was a bonanza for Boston and Rouse.

This was the first of a series of major downtown developments for Rouse and the beginning of a new era for American cities. Shopping was now perceived as theater, as a place for entertainment, with street performers and musicians. Shopping no longer was a goal-oriented process of setting out to buy a specific object, but an activity with random excitement involved in unexpected "impulse" purchases. When it was combined with a wide range of food and entertainment choices, it could provide a family outing for an entire day in a safe and secure setting among happy throngs of neighbors or tourists. The predominance of food bars, snack carousels, and restaurants was entirely intentional. "Next to sun and fire," Jane Thompson, the architect's partner, declared, "food is our most potent symbol of the life-sustaining forces, offering the warmth, protection, and nurturing that we need. A display of food gives pleasure and reassurance," she added, pointing to the ritualization of eating that takes place at all known festive occasions and holidays.

In New York City, developers were quick to seize on the commercial viability that shopping as entertainment could provide. Ada Louise Huxtable, commenting in *The New York Times* in 1978, said: "New York builders are notoriously adept at formulating a package that satisfies the letter of the law and does the least to fulfill what city planners had in mind." Under the new "incentive" zoning laws, it was possible to select from a number of options that provided special public amenities —plazas, gardens, neighborhood features—in exchange for increased building size. Up went some gargantuan towers that provided more rentable space and income for the developers, along with some public areas at ground level. Some of these developers made special efforts. Citicorp was one, commissioning Boston architect Hugh Stubbins to design midtown New York's Citicorp Tower, with its arcades of indoor shops (The Market) and a great skylit public entertainment space for concerts in its atrium. It was an example of going well beyond the minimum specifications to create a lively space for pedestrians. By the early 1980s, there were at least ten public spaces in new towers in midtown. Mrs. Huxtable called one on 57th Street, the Galleria, an "aborted effort," while Olympic Tower on Fifth Avenue was a "near copout." However, under public pressure to deliver what had been promised, modifications were made, developers saw reason in reaching out further to the public and,

In Coconut Grove, Florida, Kenneth Treister enhances the shopping mall with arts and crafts.

for the most part, the amenities improved the enjoyability of Manhattan. Cities all over the country, from Niagara Falls to Minneapolis, San Francisco to Houston, followed the prescription. In Coconut Grove, Miami, architect Kenneth Treister involved local artists and craftspeople in the construction of an elaborate multiblock development of shops, restaurants, and a hotel called Mayfair in the Grove.

These retail concepts made the concrete shoeboxes and asphalt-paved parking lots of the normal suburban shopping centers look like deprived environmental zones. From the raves in Boston, Rouse went on to bring his unique show to the waterfront in Baltimore. Here, on the disused and dilapidated harbor side, long ago abandoned by cargo ships, he and architect Benjamin Thompson created another downtown civic attraction called Harborplace. The premise was the same: "Settings for festive human interaction, made of food and clothes as well as buildings," according to Thompson. In Baltimore there were no existing old buildings to renovate, but Thompson produced an attractive feeling of pleasure pavilions, with detailing derived from romantic boathouses, ferry terminals, and bandstands, all adorned with colorful flags flying in the wind.

Rouse and Thompson likened their shopping malls to Arab bazaars, as places for social gatherings and exchange. But despite such admirable social intentions, it wasn't long before the critics raised objections to what was becoming tagged as the Faneuilization of America, particularly when Rouse set his sights on the historic South Street Seaport in Manhattan. The Rouse malls were too "sanitized," they removed the seedy dilapidation that many people found picturesque! Much of the criticism came from the architectural and design community, who had not yet seen the light. Rouse's bottom-line statistics showed that this was the kind of urban environment that people wanted—by 1981 retailers were making $300 per square foot per annum in sales.

Among the younger generation of designers, David Slovic, in Philadelphia, was one who picked up on the inherent sameness of the approaches proposed by those members of the design community representing the establishment, who were unimpressed by the idea of involving the user in the design process. "Today's debate," he pointed out in 1982, when he was named by The Architectural League of New York as an Emerging Voice, "is the Post-Modern alternative to the Modern style. The Post-Modern movement reverses the stylistic propositions of Modern architecture, reintroducing historical references, mass, defined rooms, variety in color, ornament and decoration. As an issue, the debate still centers only on aesthetic questions. The role of the architect in society and solutions to urban needs go not only unanswered but even unasked. Today's ideology is concerned with the subjectivity and the autonomy of culture, dwelling on the private life and the individual rather than the public life and citizen, on personal interests rather than concern with the general well-being. The architectural projects designed on aesthetic criteria only, making architecture as objects, can be just as uncomfortable and alienating as the Modern movement buildings. This concern for aesthetics and style, whether Modern or Post-Modern, is too narrow to produce substantial work. Architecture is an interdisciplinary act that encompasses all of life, affects all of our experiences and makes references to every level of our aesthetic existence." He went on to emphasize that professionals should establish goals for architecture that articulate not the method or style of design but the user of design as a factor necessary to the improvement of society and its environment.

Slovic put the hands-on concept of Process Architecture into his commissions. At the Old Pine Street Community Center in Philadelphia, the users were directly involved throughout the entire project. As a means of physically embodying this relationship they were asked to participate in the sidewalk tile design outside the building, working together to create a kind of "friendship quilt" of different motifs. For the Student Union at Temple University, he talked to the students to find out their preferences—the result was far from the usual, bland institutional environment and no more expensive to implement. It was not long before Slovic's work was noticed by urban and suburban developers, Rouse among them. Throughout the 1980s he was busy designing shopping malls and food courts—light-filled, lively, urban public spaces that offered a variety of fast foods—and they were often additional amenities to existing shopping malls that needed upgrading. He found ideas, he said, from city streets, sidewalk cafés and from looking at old

David Slovic involves the user in projects as a method of improving society and its environment. The Cherry Hill Food Court (*top*) brings emotional responses to the suburban shopping mall. The Student Union at Temple University (*bottom*) was designed to brighten an institutional building.

Under heavy criticism, the proposed development of New York's Columbus Circle with mixed-use building was stalled, first with an overscale project (*top left*) by Moshe Safdie and secondly with a less bulky building (*top right*) by David Childs of Skidmore, Owings & Merrill. Television City, an ambitious plan for a mile-high skyscraper and companion high-rises (*center*) by Helmut Jahn for developer Donald Trump was dropped because of neighborhood protest. An office-block addition (*bottom*) to the Guggenheim Museum by Gwathmey Siegel Associates met opposition from citizens objecting to skyline views from Central Park.

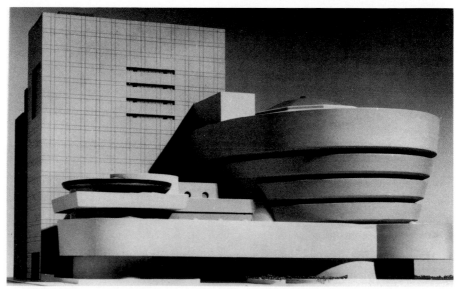

buildings with large public spaces, such as hotels and railway stations, ballrooms, and even automats that were used and loved in the past.

By the end of the 1980s, research studies noted that there was no way for developers to move forward with a project without polling popular opinion. This was finally concluded after a series of public protests in Manhattan: against Westway, a super-highway along the Hudson River; against a proposed overscale development at Columbus Circle that threatened to put Central Park in shadow; against a 100-acre development of high-rise buildings proposed by Donald Trump on the West Side railway yards, which was perceived by the public as overcrowding the neighborhood and stressing an already overstressed public transportation system; against colossal additions to the Marcel Breuer-designed Whitney and the Frank Lloyd Wright-designed Guggenheim museums, which were seen as violations of the existing structures and possible blights on the skyline. In every case, citizens spoke up to fight off "progress." The neighborhood group opposing Donald Trump raised more than $500,000 for their campaign, in which they employed lawyers and engineers to challenge aspects of the project that they described as "a monstrous phalanx of monstrous skyscrapers looming up against the sky." When the developer was forced to abandon his plan to build the tallest skyscraper in the world, designed by Helmut Jahn, Thomas Lueck in *The New York Times* noted: "It may reflect a new level of political sophistication among those opposed to large-scale real-estate development throughout New York City."

To West Side residents like Betty Friedan, leader of the feminist revolution, the new mood was reminiscent of the 1960s, when women's rights were an issue. "There's an energy level, a real commitment to fight," she said. Through opposition from the Municipal Art Society, developer Mortimer Zuckerman's Columbus Circle project was tied up in the courts from its inception in 1985 until the time this book went to press in 1989. During the course of the debate, Zuckerman dropped his original design for the building—along with his architect Moshe Safdie—for a less bulky project by Skidmore, Owings & Merrill architect David Childs. And the Design Process Task Force was established by Mayor Edward Koch in 1988 to mediate in the dispute. The Task Force's objective was an ongoing one: to avoid pitfalls in the future by taking design elements into consideration before, rather than after, the fact. The tide had turned on rampant growth, noted *The New York Times* architecture critic Paul Goldberger.

The process of public participation was also stridently called for in the office workplace. Studies done by the Louis Harris survey group for Steelcase, the nation's largest office environment company, and the Buffalo Organization for Social and Technological Innovation showed consistently that the workforce wanted to be part of the decision-making process. The job environment provided a sense of satisfaction that far

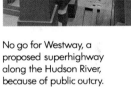

No go for Westway, a proposed superhighway along the Hudson River, because of public outcry.

From *Think* magazine, the IBM in-house publication: An employee's child sees a more organized urban plan, with solar-energized buildings, car-pool lanes, and most of the roadway given over to bicycles.

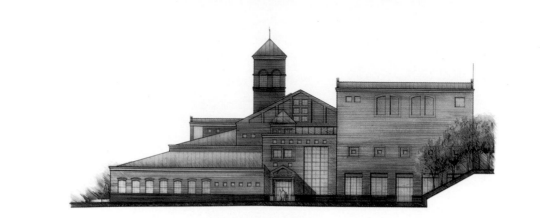

EAST ELEVATION

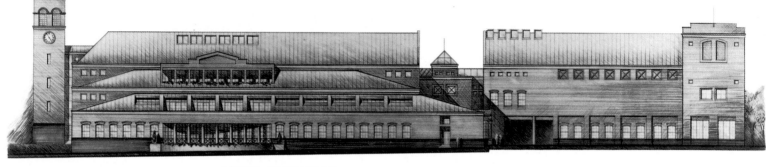

SOUTH ELEVATION

NORTH ELEVATION

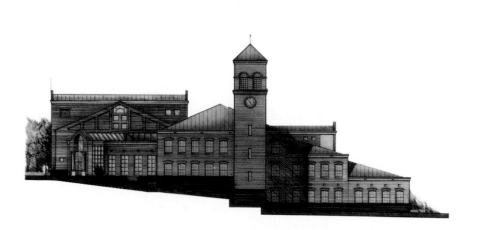

WEST ELEVATION

outweighed monetary compensation and other benefits. Harris' polls also indicated that management had some way to go before closing this gap. But improvements were steadily reported as the 1980s came to a close.

Essential to the information society also were new measures relating to the health quality of the indoor environment. These had proved necessary since Environmental Protection Agency surveys had shown that Americans spent 90 percent of their time indoors, with exposure to high-risk pollutants that exceed outdoor levels by 200 to 500 percent. "Worker's right-to-know" programs under federal OSHA laws demanded accountability and public disclosures about life-threatening and hazardous substances in the workplace from radon, asbestos, formaldehyde, pesticides, cigarette smoke, bacteria, lead in drinking water, and other less well-known hazards. Employee complaints about indoor air pollution and thermal discomfort, causing ailments ranging from skin rashes, headaches, sore throats, nausea and chronic indigestion, were a factor of poor ventilation, according to one expert, who said that as many as one out of every three office buildings had no fresh air at all and nearly half had "glot-gutted" ductwork. The National Organization of Working Women, together with the Service Employees International Union, launched a nationwide campaign for state regulations on three problem areas for clerical workers: guidelines on visual safety, including appropriate lighting; musculoskeletal concerns on height, location of computer equipment, adequate foot rest, and seating; and stress and environmental factors such as noise, ventilation, humidity, and temperature.

The American Institute of Architects, in a lengthy and comprehensive report on the state of the profession called *Vision 2000; Trends Shaping Architecture's Future* reported in May 1988 on twenty-seven "surprise free" trends forecast to the end of the century, reinforcing the strong surge in public participation. The future promised "a scenario that is demanding but positive." A renewal of social idealism, together with a widespread determination to "take responsibility" for solving problems, were among the most potent societal aspects of the forecast. "We expect a new kind of leadership will arise in many fields—both realistic and idealistic, achievement-oriented yet socially conscious—transcending old debates, creating new visions of future possibilities."

Included in the wisdom imparted to the nation by Thomas Jefferson, a distinguished architect and perceiver of the need for high-quality design to be present in every aspect of life, were these words: "I know of no safe depository of the ultimate powers of society, but the people themselves: and if we think them not enlightened enough to exercise their control with a wholesome discretion, the remedy is not to take it from them, but to inform their discretion." Of all the four tendencies outlined in this twenty-year review, Process Design calls for the closest examination and the most fervent development.

Sign of the times. A library in Massachusetts designed by Mark Mitchell and Liviu Marza includes a room for the homeless close to the toilets and a day-care center for children.

SOURCE LIST OF ARCHITECTS AND DESIGNERS

This directory of architects and designers who have been influential in the past two decades and are continuing to be leaders of substance is a broad-based selection. By reason of limited space, it does not include many others who are accomplished in the field.

WILLIAM ADAMS William Adams Architects, 1436½ Third Street Mall, Santa Monica, CA 90404   (213) 458-9397

A highly talented new-wave designer, Adams has won numerous awards for his cool, reductive interiors for residential and commercial clients.

DAVIS B. ALLEN Associate Partner/Senior Interior Designer, Skidmore, Owings & Merrill, 220 East 42nd Street, New York, NY 10017   (212) 309-9500

Credited with being, since 1950, the éminence grise behind all Skidmore, Owings & Merrill's interior design projects. Allen worked with Florence Knoll in the 1950s. He has designed numerous products for furniture companies, including Stendig, GF, and Bernhardt.

EMILIO AMBASZ 636 Broadway, New York, NY 10012 (212) 420-8850

Born in Argentina, Ambasz became curator of design at New York's Museum of Modern Art at the early age of 27. Between 1970 and 1976, he brought the museum a number of important exhibitions. Since opening his own practice, he has received numerous international awards for his work, which spans architecture, interiors, and industrial design. He is known for his Vertebra adjustable chair, designed with Giancarlo Piretti.

ROSS ANDERSON Partner, Anderson/Schwartz, 40 Hudson Street, New York, NY 10013   (212) 608-0185

In partnership with Fred Schwartz, Anderson runs a bicoastal design firm specializing in architectural and interior design for both residential and commercial projects.

EDWARD LARRABEE BARNES Edward Larrabee Barnes/ John M. Y. Lee, Architects, 320 West 13th Street, New York, NY 10014   (212) 929-3131

Architect of numerous major buildings in the Modern idiom, including the Dallas Museum of Art, the IBM New York Office Tower and Plaza Garden, and the Equitable Life Assurance headquarters in New York, Barnes has received over thirty national awards for his work.

ANDREW BATEY Dean, School of Architectural Studies, California College of Arts and Crafts, 1700 Seventeenth Street, San Francisco, CA 94103   (415) 864-0733

The firm of Batey and Mack received broad acclaim before Batey dissolved his partnership with Mark Mack to serve as dean at the California College of Arts and Crafts, Oakland, California, where he is cultivating a more reverent approach to the study of architecture through the integration of interior, architectural, graphic, and industrial design.

THOMAS H. BEEBY   Principal, Hammond Beeby and Babka, Architects, 1126 North State Street, Chicago, IL 60610 (312) 649-9300

Following Cesar Pelli as dean of architecture at Yale in 1985, Beeby maintains a busy practice in Chicago and, in 1988, won the invitational competition to design the new Chicago Library. He is known for Classical interpretations.

WARD BENNETT   1 West 72nd Street, New York, NY 10024 (212) 580-1358

A renowned designer of interiors and products, Bennett created high-quality textiles and furniture for Brickel between 1963 and 1988. His glass, china, and silverware designs are in the permanent collection of the Museum of Modern Art, New York.

KENT BLOOMER   Professor of Architectural Design, and Director, Undergraduate Studies, Yale University School of Architecture, New Haven, CT 06520   (203) 432-2294

A highly respected educator, Bloomer has received wide attention for both his architectural and sculptural projects. He is principal author, with Charles Moore, of *Body, Memory, and Architecture,* Yale University Press, 1977.

MARIO BUATTA   120 East 80th Street, New York, NY 10021 (212) 988-6811

Known as the Prince of Chintz, Buatta has achieved a significant national reputation for residential design. Among his most important commissions were fifty rooms in Blair House, the official guest house for the president's visitors in Washington, DC, completed in 1988.

JOHN BURGEE   John Burgee Architects, 885 Third Avenue, New York, NY 10022   (212) 751-7440

A partner with Philip Johnson from 1967, Burgee assumed senior partnership of the firm in 1983. Together, between 1970 and 1989, Johnson and Burgee designed well over twenty-five high-rise buildings all over the country, most of them with Gerald D. Hines as the developer. Their most notable is the famous AT&T tower in New York.

HENRY N. COBB   Founding Principal, I. M. Pei & Partners, 600 Madison Avenue, New York, NY 10022   (212) 751-3122

Since the formation of the Pei firm in 1955, Cobb has contributed actively and continuously, working on numerous major projects that include the Allied Bank Tower in Dallas and the block-long Commerce Square project in Philadelphia. He has coupled this creativity with active teaching appointments, and from 1980 to 1985 he served as chairman of the Department of Architecture at the Harvard Graduate School of Design.

PATRICIA CONWAY   President, Kohn Pedersen Fox Conway Associates, 251 West 57th Street, New York, NY 10019 (212) 397-1100

From a background of journalism and urban planning, Conway took over as principal partner in the interior design firm owned by Kohn Pederson Fox in 1978. She was named *Interiors* Designer of the Year in 1987 for projects including the interiors of Procter and Gamble and the Equitable Life Assurance headquarters.

RAUL DE ARMAS Partner in Charge of Interior Design, Skidmore, Owings & Merrill, 220 East 42nd Street, New York, NY 10017 (212) 309-9500

Born in Cuba, de Armas became one of SOM's forty-four partners in 1979, after twelve years with the firm. He was named *Interiors* Designer of the Year in 1984, on the basis of his ability to adapt state-of-the-art technology to the needs of corporate and financial institutions.

ORLANDO DIAZ-AZCUY Orlando Diaz-Azcuy Designs, 305 Grant Avenue, 8th Floor, San Francisco, CA 94108 (415) 788-3058

One of the West Coast's most significant award-winning interior and product designers, Diaz-Azcuy worked as design principal for the firm of Gensler & Associates, Architects, before opening his own studio in 1985. In 1982, he was named *Interiors* Designer of the Year.

NIELS DIFFRIENT 879 North Salem Road, Ridgefield, CT 06877 (203) 438-5660

A preeminent industrial designer, Diffrient was with Henry Dreyfuss Associates for twenty-five years before he opened his own consulting practice in 1981. He is renowned for his research into human dimensions and his award-winning seating designs for Knoll and Sunar-Hauserman.

ROBERT DOORNICK President, Future Designs, 611 Broadway, Suite 422A, New York, NY 10012 (212) 228-0392

Trained in engineering and child psychology, Doornick is president of the interior design division of International Robotics, a firm that specializes in the interaction between humans and machines.

JOSEPH PAUL D'URSO D'Urso Designs, 80 West 40th Street, New York, NY 10018 (212) 869-9313

Known for his high-tech interior designs and products for Knoll, D'Urso maintained a small, prestigious office in the 1970s and 1980s. He won a Prix de Rome in 1987.

PETER EISENMAN Eisenman Architects, 40 West 25th Street, New York, NY 10010 (212) 645-1400

Founder and director of the Institute for Architecture and Urban Studies in New York between 1967 and 1982, Eisenman is widely recognized for his contribution to the linguistic theory of architectural design. He is the winner of numerous awards as well as a leading educator and author. Among honors he has received is the Stone Lion, awarded at the Third International Architectural Biennale in Venice.

ARTHUR ERICKSON President, Arthur Erickson Associates, 125 North Robertson Boulevard, Los Angeles, CA 90048 (213) 278-1915

With a reputation as one of North America's most distinguished architects, Erickson operates offices in Vancouver, Toronto, Los Angeles, and Saudi Arabia. The firm won a competition for the eleven-acre California Plaza project in Los Angeles in 1980. Erickson has won many honors and awards.

FREDERICK FISHER Frederick Fisher Architect, 1422 Second Street, Santa Monica, CA 90401 (213) 451-1767

After working for Frank O. Gehry, Fisher opened his own office in 1978. He has won several awards for his domestic architecture and interior design.

BERNARDO FORT-BRESCIA   Arquitectonica, 2151 LeJeune Road, Suite 300, Coral Gables, FL 33134   (305) 442-9381

Fort-Brescia, working in partnership with his wife, Laurinda Speare, since 1977, has made Arquitectonica known for abstract designs that integrate cost-efficient construction techniques with the personality of the community. These works have captured widespread public attention, won numerous design awards, and left their mark in New York, Chicago, and San Francisco.

FRANK O. GEHRY   Frank O. Gehry & Associates, 15200B Cloverfield Boulevard, Santa Monica, CA 90404 (213) 939-6088

Recognized as the West Coast's most inventive architect, Gehry opened his practice in 1962. Among his numerous award-winning projects are his own house and the Temporary Contemporary Museum in Los Angeles. He is known for his "brutalist" combinations of materials, including chain-link fence, concrete, and plywood.

M. ARTHUR GENSLER, JR.   Gensler & Associates Architects, 550 Kearny Street, San Francisco, CA 94108 (415) 433-3700

Founder of the nation's largest firm specializing in commercial interior planning and design, Gensler expanded from one West Coast office in 1965 to eight nationwide in 1989. The firm now has over 650 employees.

SIDNEY PHILIP GILBERT   President and Chief Executive Officer, SPGA Architects Group Inc., 65 Bleecker Street, New York, NY 10012   (212) 505-6300

Founder of Architects, Designers, and Planners for Social Responsibility in 1980, Gilbert served as its president in 1988. He has contributed to improved Soviet/American relations in the design community through the exchange of publications as well as professional tours and lectures. He runs a large interior design firm with over 400 employees specializing in commercial work.

ROMALDO GIURGOLA   Partner, Mitchell/Giurgola Architects. 170 West 97th St. New York, NY 10025 (212) 663-4000

Born in Italy, Giurgola formed a partnership with Ehrman Burkman Mitchell, Jr., in 1958 in Philadelphia. The firm received many notable commissions and in 1979 was awarded first place in an international design competition that had 329 entries for the new Parliament House in Canberra, Australia—one of the largest projects to be built in the world during the 1980s. Giurgola has received over forty major awards for his buildings.

MICHAEL GRAVES   Michael Graves Architect, 341 Nassau Street, Princeton, NJ 08540   (609) 924-6409

Known as the leader of Post-Modernism, Graves has been on the faculty of the School of Architecture at Princeton since 1962. Notable among his designs are the Humana headquarters in Louisville, the Portland, Oregon civic building, and the expansion of the Whitney Museum in New York. He has also designed interiors and products for SunarHauserman and many residences for private clients.

CAROL GROH   Principal, GN Associates, 595 Madison Avenue, New York, NY 10022   (212) 935-2900

After an eleven-year apprenticeship at Skidmore, Owings & Merrill, Groh opened her own firm, GN Associates, in 1979. She specializes in corporate design and was named *Interiors* Designer of the Year in 1988.

CHARLES GWATHMEY   Principal, Gwathmey Siegel &
Associates, Architects, 475 Tenth Avenue, New York, NY 10018
(212) 947-1240

Gwathmey worked with Edward Larrabee Barnes before
founding his own practice in 1966. The firm was renamed when
Robert Siegel joined in 1968, and in 1970 Gwathmey became
the youngest recipient of the Brunner Prize for his significant
contribution to architecture as an art. The firm has won
numerous awards. Gwathmey has lectured at many univer-
sities and colleges.

PAUL HAIGH   Haigh Space Architecture + Design,
27 West 20th Street, New York, NY 10011   (212) 691-2017

An all-around British-trained architect, interior designer,
and product designer, Haigh has won numerous awards for
projects ranging from stores to private houses. His product designs for Bieffeplast, Conde/House, Bernhardt, Knoll,
and others have won him acclaim. He has taught at Parsons
School of Design and at the Fashion Institute of Technology
in New York.

FRANCES HALSBAND   Partner, R. M. Kliment & Frances
Halsband Architects, 255 West 26 Street,
New York, NY 10001   (212) 243-7400

In partnership with her husband, Robert Klimet, since 1972,
Halsband has risen to prominence in a profession traditionally dominated by men. She became President of The Architectural League of New York in 1985, holding a four-year term.
The firm is known for its strong interest in designing custom
furniture for clients, which led to furniture designs for Cad-
sana in 1988.

MARK HAMPTON   Mark Hampton Inc., 654 Madison
Avenue, New York, NY 10021   (212) 753-4110

Widely respected for his tasteful restorations of period interiors, Hampton has worked on the White House for President
and Mrs. Reagan; the vice president's headquarters; Blair
House; Gracie Mansion, the mayor's official residence in New
York; and the governor of New York's official residence in
Albany. He is also known for his furniture, adapted from late-
eighteenth and nineteenth-century designs.

HUGH HARDY   Partner, Hardy Holzman Pfeiffer Associates
Partnership, 902 Broadway, New York, NY 10010
(212) 677-6030

Hardy is widely known as a designer and renovator of theaters,
for the integration of art and architecture, and for the ingenious use of commonplace materials. His firm was responsible
for the restoration in 1988 of the famous Rainbow Room, an
Art Deco landmark in Rockefeller Center, New York.

JOHN HEJDUK   Dean, The Irwin S. Chanin School of
Architecture of The Cooper Union, Cooper Square,
New York, NY 10003   (212) 254-6397

Since 1975, Hejduk has been teaching architecture through its
interrelationships with other art forms. He has had numerous
exhibitions of his drawings and contributed to major shows
abroad, including the Venice Biennale and Milan Triennale,
and he has received many honors.

CRAIG HODGETTS   Hodgetts and Fung Design Associates,
1750 Berkeley Street, Santa Monica, CA 90404
(213) 829-1969

An experimental designer, Hodgetts has worked on exhibitions, films, entertainment events and even commercials,
bringing his own idiosyncratic architectural narrative to
these projects. He has also designed unusual private residences in the Los Angeles area.

STEVEN HOLL Steven Holl Architects, 133 West 19th Street, 10th floor, New York, NY 10011 (212) 989-0918

In 1978, Holl founded his New York firm on the principle that no architectural project should be straitjacketed by the dictates of a specific style. Instead, each project should reflect the client's spirit and individuality. He has worked on many private residences, designed products, and is an associate professor of architecture at Columbia University, New York.

MALCOLM HOLZMAN Hardy Holzman Pfeiffer Associates, 902 Broadway, New York, NY 10010 (212) 677-6030

As one of the founding principals of HHPA, Holzman has been partner in charge of a variety of corporate, commercial, educational and arts projects, including the Best Products headquarters and the Willard Hotel in Washington, D.C. He has served as a Visiting Professor of Design at Yale University and lectures frequently to professional and lay audiences on design for the visual and performing arts.

LUCIA HOWARD Ace Architects, 5237 College Avenue, Oakland, CA 94618 (415) 658-2543

Principal of her own firm since 1978, Howard, with partner David Weingarten, is noted in the Bay Area for retail and office interiors that are a blend of fantasy and artistry.

COY HOWARD Coy Howard and Company, 2928 Nebraska Avenue, Santa Monica, CA 90404 (213) 453-1789

An all rounder, Howard has produced a full range of residences, office buildings, shopping centers, exhibitions, industrial and furniture designs, films, and graphic communications. He has been the recipient of awards and the subject of several shows.

FRANK ISRAEL Franklin D. Israel Design Associates, 254 South Robertson Boulevard, Suite 205, Beverly Hills, CA 90211 (213) 652-8087

Opening his own practice in 1979, Israel's renovations in the Los Angeles area have brought him praise from both architectural journals and clients. He is associate professor of architecture at the University of California, Los Angeles.

HUGH NEWELL JACOBSEN 2529 P Street N.W., Washington, DC 20007 (202) 337-5200

A leading architectural influence in Washington, D.C., Jacobsen supervised the restoration of The Renwick Gallery. He has built houses in areas ranging from Washington, D.C. to the Caribbean that have won him more than eighty awards.

HELMUT JAHN Murphy/Jahn Architects, 35 East Wacker Drive, Chicago, IL 60601 (312) 427-7300

Known as Chicago's enfant terrible in the 1970s, Jahn rose to become a principal of the firm Murphy/Jahn in 1981. His high-rises in many far-flung locales are marked by his exuberant approach to the use of glass and high technology. They have earned him over fifty awards.

PHILIP JOHNSON John Burgee Architects, 885 Third Avenue, New York, NY 10022 (212) 751-7440

Johnson has been a prominent personality in the world of design since 1932, when, as a young director in the Department of Architecture at New York's Museum of Modern Art, he and Henry-Russell Hitchcock launched the International Style. Johnson was instrumental in bringing Modernism to America. His work with Mies van der Rohe includes the Seagram Building in New York, and he has numerous other buildings to his credit. Among the most famous is his own Glass House, built in 1949 in Connecticut, and the AT&T headquarters building in New York.

MICHAEL KALIL Kalil Studio, 307 East 76th Street, New York, NY 10021 (212) 861-1467

Having studied weaving, sculpture, architecture, theology, and design, Kalil set up his own independent design studio in 1971. He has taught at several leading design schools, worked for a select number of prestigious clients, lectured all over the world, and is regarded as a leading philosopher/designer. He has been under contract to NASA since 1983 as Arrangements Consultant on the Space Station's Interior Architecture.

PAUL KENNON CRS Sirrine Inc, 1111 West Loop South, P.O. Box 22427, Houston, TX 77227 (713) 552-2193

Trained at Cranbrook, Kennon worked for seven years as a senior designer with Eero Saarinen. He then joined the Houston firm of Caudill, Rowlett, Scott, known for its wide-ranging projects and its strong interest in ecological architecture. In 1983 it acquired Environmental Planning and Research of San Francisco, an interiors firm, and then Sirrine. It is now a public company quoted on the New York Stock Exchange, with 15 offices and 2,971 employees. Scott Strasser, director of interior design in the Dallas office, was named *Interiors* Designer of the Year in 1989.

ROBERT M. KLIMENT Partner, R. M. Kliment & Frances Halsband Architects, 255 West 26 Street, New York, NY 10001 (212) 243-7400

Having been influenced by the Philadelphia School while at Mitchell/Giurgola's office during the 1960s, Kliment opened his own office in New York in 1972 with Frances Halsband, and together they have formed a team that has received acclaim for residential and commercial architecture, urban planning, and interior design with a range of public and private clients.

FRANCISCO KRIPACZ President, Arthur Erickson Associates Architects, and Principal in Charge of the firm's Los Angeles office, 125 North Robertson Boulevard, Los Angeles, CA 90048 (213) 278-1915

Kripacz has been an associate of Arthur Erickson for more than 20 years, with responsibility for many of the Erickson office's interior design projects. He was named *Interiors* Designer of the Year in 1985.

JACK LENOR LARSEN 41 East 11th Street, New York, NY 10003 (212) 674-3993

A noted authority on textile design, Larsen has been designing and supplying textiles to major design firms for thirty years. His collections are inspired by ideas from every corner of the world. More recently he has diversified into carpet design, tableware, and furniture. He is author of six books, including *Interlacing: The Elemental Fabric* with Betty Freudenheim in 1986 and winner of numerous awards and honors for his contribution to the development of textile history.

JOHN MING-YEE LEE Edward Larrabee Barnes/John M. Y. Lee Architects, 320 West 13th Street, New York, NY 10014 (212) 929-3131

Partner in the New York firm with Barnes since 1967, Lee has participated in nine major design projects, including the New York headquarters of the Asia Society, the Wichita Art Museum, and the Museum of New Mexico, Santa Fe.

SARAH TOMERLIN LEE   President, Tom Lee Limited,
136 East 57th Street, New York, NY 10022   (212) 421-4433

A former editor-in-chief of *House Beautiful* magazine, Lee turned to interior design in partnership with her husband, Tom Lee, and has continued the business since his death in 1971. Her notable projects have included hotels such as the Helmsley Palace in New York, The Willard Hotel in Washington, D.C.; and the Saturnia Spa in Coral Gables, Florida.

DAVID LEWIS   Founder-Partner, UDA Architects, 1133 Penn Avenue, Pittsburgh, PA 15222   (412) 765-1133

After emigrating from Great Britain, Lewis set up his own architecture and urban design planning firm in Pittsburgh in 1964. He is well known in academic circles, having held various professorships at Yale and Carnegie Mellon. He has been a member of the AIA National Committee for Regional/ Urban Design Assistance Teams since 1975 and is author of R/UDAT's policy statement.

ROBERT MANGURIAN   Principal, Studio Works,
4 Rose Avenue, Venice, CA 90291   (213) 399-3505

Founded in 1969 with Craig Hodgetts, Studio Works has been responsible for some leading-edge designs that have won numerous architectural awards. They include the Clos Pegase Winery and work on the conversion of Hadrian's Villa to current archeological standards. He is director of the graduate program at SCI-ARC and has lectured at many colleges.

THOM MAYNE   Principal, Morphosis Architects,
1718 22nd Street, Santa Monica, CA 90404   (213) 453-2247

A founding member of the small design firm Morphosis, Mayne has become known for an idiosyncratic approach representing a West Coast style. He is the director of SCI-ARC, and was a Prix de Rome winner in 1987.

MICHAEL McCOY   Co-Chairman, Interiors and Industrial Design Department, Cranbrook Academy of Art,
500 Lone Pine Road, Box 801, Bloomfield Hills, MI 48013
(313) 645-3300

In addition to his responsibilities at Cranbrook, McCoy is a partner in the firm of McCoy & McCoy Associates. He is known throughout the design community for injecting symbolic meanings into interior, furniture, and technological product designs for such firms as Philips, Knoll, Artifort, and Formica Corporation.

KATHERINE McCOY   Co-Chairman, Interior and Industrial Design Department, Cranbrook Academy of Art,
500 Lone Pine Road, Box 801, Bloomfield Hills, MI 48013
(313) 645-3300

In addition to her academic responsibilities, McCoy is a partner in the firm of McCoy & McCoy Associates. She has won countless awards for her graphics and signage.

MARGARET McCURRY   Tigerman McCurry, 444 North Wells, Chicago, IL 60610   (312) 644-5880

Formerly with the Chicago office of Skidmore, Owings & Merrill, McCurry opened her own practice before joining up with Stanley Tigerman. She is responsible for the firm's interior design projects, which range from large public buildings to private residential jobs.

ANDREW MacNAIR Manhattan Studio for Architecture, 10 Gramercy Park South, New York, NY 10010 (212) 529-9040

As a fellow of the Institute for Architecture & Urban Studies, New York, between 1967 and 1982, MacNair was responsible for an extraordinarily significant series of programs and exhibitions as well as for publication of the magazine *Skyline*. He was appointed professor of design at Parsons School of Design in 1983 and became chairman of the Department of Architecture at Pratt in 1983. In 1986, he resigned to open his own practice and to publish the magazine *Architectures*. He has had numerous exhibitions of his theoretical work all over the world.

RICHARD MEIER Richard Meier & Partners, 475 Tenth Avenue, New York, NY 10018 (212) 967-6060

Named as one of the "New York Five" architects in 1970, Meier has pursued a Modernist approach to design that has earned him international acclaim and commissions. His works have included major private houses, products for Knoll, and—most notably—several museums built during the 1970s and 1980s. The new High Museum in Atlanta stands out among these. He is currently at work on the Getty Museum in Los Angeles, a ten-year project.

EDWARD I. MILLS Voorsanger & Mills Associates, 246 West 38 Street, New York, NY 10018 (212) 302-6464

Formerly with I. M. Pei, Davis Brody, and Richard Meier before joining Bartholomew Voorsanger in partnership, Mills is also a well-known professor, lecturer, and guest critic. His work includes high-quality residences and boutiques, as well as unique offices and furniture design.

CHARLES MOORE Moore Ruble Yudell Architects & Planners, 1640 Nineteenth Street, Santa Monica, CA 90404 (213) 829-9923

After Moore was dean of the School of Architecture at Yale from 1965 to 1970, he pursued a busy practice with Moore Grover Harper/Centerbrook in Essex, Connecticut, which designed many private residences, art galleries, public projects, and housing developments. In 1975 Moore became a professor of architecture at University of California, Los Angeles. He has been associated with the school's practice arm, Urban Innovation Group, since 1975 and opened a West Coast office with John Ruble and Buzz Yudell in 1977. He is now O'Neill Ford Professor of Architecture at the University of Texas at Austin.

ERIC OWEN MOSS 3964 Ince Boulevard, Culver City, CA 90230 (213) 839-1199

Winner of several awards for his sensitive architectural designs, Moss opened his own firm in 1976. He is on the board of directors at SCI-ARC.

BRIAN ALFRED MURPHY BAM Construction Design Inc., 14800 Corona Del Mar, Pacific Palisades, CA 90272 (213) 459-7547

Named as one of the Emerging Voices by the Architectural League in 1986, Murphy is known for his ad hoc nondesign approach, which is doubtless an outgrowth of his apprenticeship in the construction industry.

DAVID NIXON Partner, Future Systems Consultants, 1103 South Hudson Avenue, Los Angeles, CA 90019 (213) 938-8528

David Nixon established Future Systems with Jan Kaplicky in 1979, seeking to transcend convention through innovative approaches to design/construction technology.

IEOH MING PEI I. M. Pei & Partners, 600 Madison Avenue, New York, NY 10022   (212) 751-3122

Having founded his own firm in 1955, I. M. Pei has been a significant force in architectural design for more than thirty years. His contributions have included major museums such as the East Wing of the National Gallery in Washington, D.C., numerous high rises, and hotels all over the world. A most controversial project was his addition to the Louvre in Paris completed in 1988.

CESAR PELLI Cesar Pelli & Associates, 1056 Chapel Street, New Haven, CT 06510   (203) 777-2515

Pelli was born in Argentina and studied at the University of Illinois. He then worked with Eero Saarinen and served as dean of the School of Architecture at Yale from 1977 to 1984. His accomplishments include the Pacific Design Center in Los Angeles, the Commons in Columbus, Indiana, the Battery Park City towers in New York, and the residential tower and museum expansion of the Museum of Modern Art, New York.

CHARLES PFISTER President, The Pfister Partnership, 40 Hotaling Place, San Francisco, CA 94111   (415) 392-4455

Formerly in the San Francisco office of Skidmore, Owings & Merrill, Pfister set up his own firm in 1981. Since then has won many awards for his interiors, architecture, and product designs. He has produced furniture for Knoll, Bernhardt, Casa Bella, and Baker. In 1986, he was named *Interiors* Designer of the Year.

NORMAN PFEIFFER Hardy Holzman Pfeiffer Associates, 902 Broadway, New York, NY 10010   (212) 677-6030

One of the founding principals of HHPA, Pfeiffer heads the Los Angeles offices, established in 1986, and oversees the major West Coast projects that are ongoing, including the renovation of the Los Angeles City Hall, the expansion of the Central Library, and the Master Plan for the Los Angeles County Museum of Art.

WARREN PLATNER President, Warren Platner Associates, 18 Mitchell Drive, New Haven, CT 06511   (203) 777-6471

After completing his studies at Cornell University in New York, Platner was awarded the Prix de Rome, an Advanced Research Fulbright Award, and a Graham Foundation Award for Advanced Studies. He has been a significant force in total design, including landscaping, graphics, lighting, and furniture, for which he has won numerous international awards.

JAMES STEWART POLSHEK President, James Stewart Polshek and Partners, 320 West 13th Street, New York, NY 10014   (212) 807-7171

Dean of the Columbia School of Architecture from 1972 to 1987, Polshek also maintained a busy practice that has been responsible for numerous major civic and public projects, schools, libraries, and hospitals, many of which have won international awards. He is a co-founder of Architects, Designers and Planners for Social Responsibility, is on the executive committee of the Municipal Arts Society in New York, and is a member on the advisory board of the Center for Preservation Research at Columbia University.

JOHN C. PORTMAN President, The Portman Companies, 225 Peachtree Street, N.E., Suite 201, Atlanta, GA 30303 (404) 420-5252

Portman is a pioneer in the role of the architect/developer, and his high-rise multi-use concept has shaped numerous projects across the United States. Since 1971, his firm has become a conglomeration of eight real estate business entities with over 1,100 employees. In the late 1980s, The Portman companies initiated developments in China.

CHARLES REDMON Cambridge Seven Associates, Inc., 1050 Massachusetts Avenue, Cambridge, MA 02138 (617) 492-7000

Redmon, who joined Cambridge Seven in 1965, had progressed to managing principal by 1986. His firm has been involved in numerous large-scale projects including the Houston Design Center. He is an active participant in the AIA's Urban Planning and Design Committee as well as a chairman of the R/UDAT Task Force.

KEVIN ROCHE Principal, Kevin Roche, John Dinkeloo and Associates, P.O. Box 6127, 20 Davis Street, Hamden, CT 06517 (203) 777-7251

Roche joined Eero Saarinen and Associates in 1950 and then, after Saarinen's death in 1961, formed a partnership with John Dinkeloo in order to complete the firm's unfinished projects. Among these were the TWA terminal at JFK Airport, the St. Louis Arch, and the Deere and Company headquarters. Since that time, he has won numerous honors and built many significant structures, including the additions to the Metropolitan Museum of Art in New York.

JOSEPH L. ROSEN President, Rosen Perry Preston, Inc., 3 West 18th Street, New York, NY 10011 (212) 989-9880

After working for fifteen years with ISD Incorporated in New York, where he helped to develop numerous major corporate headquarters, Rosen opened his own firm in 1985. He was named *Interiors* Designer of the Year in 1983 and is known for his collaboration with Philip Johnson on the interiors of the AT&T Building.

MICHAEL ROTONDI Morphosis Architects, 1718 22nd Street, Santa Monica, CA 90404 (213) 453-2247

Partner with Thom Mayne in Morphosis since 1976, Rotondi has taught at SCI-ARC, Columbia University, and the University of Pennsylvania while also maintaining a busy practice specializing in southern California residential projects.

PAUL RUDOLPH President, Paul Rudolph Architect, 54 West 57th Street, New York, NY 10019 (212) 765-1450

Rudolph served as chairman of the Yale University Department of Architecture between 1958 and 1965 and is one of the nation's most prolific builders. During the last forty-two years, he has designed hundreds of private houses for clients in twenty states. He has also built high rises, schools, and other large-scale projects and has received numerous awards.

MOSHE SAFDIE Moshe Safdie and Associates, 100 Properzi Way, Somerville, MA 02143 (617) 629-2100

Following a year's work in Louis Kahn's office in Philadelphia in 1962, Safdie became the Master Planner of the 1967 World Expo in Montreal, for which he also created the widely-acclaimed model apartment project, Habitat. He opened his own practice in 1964 and has offices in Boston, Montreal, Quebec, New York, and Jerusalem. Winner of many world honors, Safdie completed three museums in Canada in the 1980s. He served as Director of the Urban Design Program at Harvard University from 1978 until 1984.

JOHN F. SALADINO   President, John F. Saladino Inc.,
305 East 63rd Street, New York, NY 10021   (212) 752-2440

Since Saladino opened his own practice in 1972, he has planned interiors and products for a wide variety of clients, taking care to humanize his designs through a sense of proportion and the use of traditional materials and forms. In 1980 he was named *Interiors* Designer of the Year.

FREDERICK SCHWARTZ   Partner, Anderson/Schwartz,
40 Hudson Street, New York, NY 10013   (212) 608-0185

After working for Skidmore, Owings & Merrill in Boston and Venturi, Rauch and Scott Brown, Schwartz opened his own firm in 1984. His projects include restaurants, apartments, and an irreverent late entry to the Chicago Tribune Tower Competition in 1980.

DENISE SCOTT BROWN   Partner, Venturi, Rauch and Scott Brown, 4236 Main Street, Philadelphia, PA 19127
(215) 487-0400

Partner in the famous Philadelphia firm since 1969, Scott Brown has been a critical figure in the adaptation of architecture to various social and political climates. She is a well-known lecturer and has earned over twenty awards for her work.

DER SCUTT   Der Scutt Architect, 44 West 28th Street,
New York, NY 10001   (212) 725-2300

A principal designer in the firm of Kahn & Jacobs/HOK between 1973 and 1975 and partner at Swanke Hayden Connell from 1976 to 1981, Scutt opened his own firm in 1981. A designer of office complexes in New York as well as abroad, his most notable achievements are the Trump Tower in New York and Trump Plaza in Atlantic City, New Jersey.

ROBERT SIEGEL   Partner, Gwathmey Siegel & Associates Architects, 475 Tenth Avenue, New York, NY 10018
(212) 947-1240.

Siegel joined the firm of Gwathmey Henderson and Siegel Architects in 1968; since then, his contributions have won numerous awards. His firm has built numerous large-scale projects, ranging from school dormitories to firehouses, as well as private houses and apartments. It won the AIA's Firm Award in 1982 for upholding the highest standards of the profession.

ALISON SKY   Partner and Co-Founder, SITE, 65 Bleecker Street, New York, NY 10012   (212) 254-8300

Since 1970, the firm of SITE has been preeminent in designing conceptual projects for various clients, including Best Products, Willi Smith, and Swatch. The firm integrates art and architecture, expressing the meaning of a project through visual narration. Its work has won numerous awards and it has been included in exhibitions all over the world.

DAVID SCOTT SLOVIC   David Slovic Associates,
1215 Locust Street, Philadelphia, PA 19107   (215) 732-7180

After working for Louis Kahn and studying at the University of Pennsylvania, Slovic founded Friday Architects/Planners in 1970, a firm that has won praise for its socially minded design concepts. Renamed David Slovic Associates in 1982, it excels in the design of shopping malls and restaurants. Slovic was named an Emerging Voice by the Architectural League in 1982. He is Henry Luce Professor of Architecture and Society at Tulane University.

PAOLO SOLERI President, Cosanti Foundation, 6433 Doubletree Road, Scottsdale, AZ 85253 (602) 948-6145

A designer and educator, Soleri has maintained an ad hoc campus in Scottsdale, where students both design and build. He has lectured all over the world, and his theoretical work has been shown at numerous exhibitions and museums.

ROBERT A. M. STERN Principal, Robert A. M. Stern Architects, 211 West 61st Street, New York, NY 10023 (212) 246-1980

Widely recognized as a prominent representative of Post-Modern and Modern Classicism in architecture, Stern has been professor of architecture at Columbia University since 1982 while also maintaining a busy practice. He has built countless houses and more recently begun to receive commissions for large-scale projects. In 1986, he was also host of an eight-hour television program entitled *Pride of Place,* intended as a popular overview of American architecture.

HUGH ASHER STUBBINS, JR. The Stubbins Associates, Inc., 1033 Massachusetts Avenue, Cambridge, MA 02138 (617) 491-6450.

During World War II, Stubbins worked at Harvard on the development of three-dimensional rendering techniques for training naval pilots. He opened his own design office in 1940 and headed the first incorporated architectural firm in Massachusetts in 1957. He has continued to be a strong force in the profession ever since. His technical ingenuity is evident in New York's Citicorp Center and the Federal Reserve Bank of Boston.

BENJAMIN THOMPSON Benjamin Thompson & Associates, Inc., One Story Street, Cambridge, MA 02138 (617) 876-4300

A pace-setting architectural firm with numerous major projects to their credit, Thompson and his wife, Jane, work together as a team. During the 1970s and 1980s, the firm worked with The Rouse Company on numerous shopping malls including Faneuil Hall, Boston, and Harborplace, Baltimore.

STANLEY TIGERMAN Principal Tigerman McCurry, 444 North Wells, Chicago, Ill 60610 (312) 644-5880

Tigerman worked for both Skidmore, Owings & Merrill, and in the office of Paul Rudolph before opening his own firm in 1962. He has authored several books, including *Versus,* and *The Architecture of Exile.* In 1980 he authored *Late Entries to the Chicago Tribune Tower Competition,* which received praise from national and international critics. As the founder of the "Chicago Seven," his work has received widespread recognition for its witty blend of sarcasm and reverence. A well-known figure in academe, Tigerman is director of the School of Architecture at the University of Illinois.

KENNETH TREISTER Kenneth Treister Architect, 3660 Battersea Road, Coconut Grove, FL. 33133 (305) 667-3170

Known for his special approach to designing major architectural developments—hotels, offices, shopping centers—in combination with local artisans and artists, Treister has tried to follow in the spirit of Frank Lloyd Wright with his approach to organic design.

BERNARD TSCHUMI   227 West 17th Street, New York, NY 10011   (212) 807-6340

An academician with a long career as a design educator, Tschumi has taught at Princeton University and The Cooper Union. In 1983, he won the international competition for the Parc de La Villette in Paris and he has received numerous awards. In 1988, he was named dean of the School of Architecture at Columbia University.

BILLIE TSIEN   Tod Williams Billie Tsien and Associates, 222 Central Park South, New York, NY 10019   (212) 582-2385

Partner with Tod Williams since 1987, Tsien has a distinguished teaching record and has won two NEA grants. She has been included in sixteen shows and brings a reductive aesthetic to residential work.

WILLIAM TURNBULL   Mr. William Turnbull Associates, Pier 1 and 1/2, The Embarcadero, San Francisco, CA 94111 (415) 986-3642

Turnbull was in partnership with Charles Moore and Don Lyndon before he opened his own firm in San Francisco in 1969. He is noted for his humanistic approach to the design of both large-scale projects and private residences.

MICHAEL JAMES VANDERBYL   Vanderbyl Design, 539 Bryant Street, San Francisco, CA 94107   (415) 543-8447

As a graphic designer and dean of the School of Design at the California College of Arts and Crafts, Oakland, California, Vanderbyl has won equal praise for his innovative approach to both interior and products design, in particular a line of textiles developed in 1987 for Esprit. Among his numerous prizes is the acclaimed IBD award for his design of the Cambridge Chair for Hickory Business Furniture in 1986.

SIM VAN DER RYN   55 Gate Five Road, Sausalito, CA 94965 (415) 332-5806

Noted for his study of ecologically functional architecture, Van der Ryn has been responsible for a variety of projects in California that have used solar energy. He was named California's State Architect in 1975 and won an award for his design of the energy-efficient State Building, named Site 1-A.

ROBERT VENTURI   Venturi, Rauch and Scott Brown, 4236 Main Street, Philadelphia PA 19127   (215) 487-0400

Considered a founder of Post-Modernism, Venturi is the author of several books, most notably *Complexity and Contradiction in Architecture* (1966) and *Learning from Las Vegas* (1972, with Denise Scott Brown and Steven Izenour). He has taught at Yale, the University of Pennsylvania, and UCLA, and his firm has built notable projects, including Woo Hall at Princeton University, the addition to Oberlin College of Music, and the addition to the National Gallery in London, a commission that was won in an international competition. Venturi has also designed numerous private residences as well as furniture for Knoll.

LELLA VIGNELLI   Vignelli Associates, 475 Tenth Avenue, New York, NY 10018   (212) 244-1919

Lella and Massimo Vignelli, who co-founded their firm in Milan, opened their New York office in 1971. Lella Vignelli is responsible for their interior and furniture designs, which have won numerous awards. The firm's work has been the subject of several television programs.

MASSIMO VIGNELLI   Vignelli Associates, 475 Tenth Avenue, New York, NY 10018   (212) 244-1919

After studying in Milan, Vignelli co-founded Unimark International Corporation in Chicago, famous for its graphic design work. He then went into partnership with Lella Vignelli, his wife. Although he was trained as an architect, Vignelli's work represents a thorough integration of the graphic arts with architecture. He has won numerous awards both in the United States and abroad.

BARTHOLOMEW VOORSANGER   Partner, Voorsanger & Mills Associates Architects, 246 West 38th Street, New York, NY 10018   (212) 302-6464

Voorsanger worked with the Canadian planning firm of Vincent Ponte and then as an associate with I. M. Pei & Partners. He opened his own firm with Edward Mills, also formerly with Pei, in 1978. The firm has been recognized for its ingenious solutions to housing problems, offices, retail stores, and furniture design.

KEVIN WALZ   Principal, Walz Design Inc., 141 Fifth Avenue, New York, NY 10010   (212) 477-2211

Trained as a fine artist, Walz was a successful painter before turning to interior and product design in 1976. He is well known in the areas of residential design, building conversion, offices and showrooms, and retail design and has received several awards for his work.

GARY S. WHITNEY   President, The Whitney Group, Inc., 1008 Barkdull Street, Houston, TX 77006   (713) 526-7382

Building on his experience as senior vice president at 3D International, where he worked for thirteen years, Whitney opened his own firm in 1987. It is one of the only architectural and interior design firms in the country to use a computer-aided design and drafting system as its primary design tool.

TOD WILLIAMS   Tod Williams Billie Tsien and Associates, 222 Central Park South, New York, NY 10019   (212) 582-2385

After working in Richard Meier's office for six years, Williams opened his own office in 1973. Since 1986 he has been in partnership with Billie Tsien. The firm is well known for its residential work.

JAMES WINES   Co-Founder and Principal SITE Projects, Inc., 65 Bleecker Street, New York, NY 10012   (212) 254-8300

A sculptor and fine arts painter, Wines spent twelve years living in Italy. His own firm, founded in 1970, has been recognized as the initiator of narrative architecture. In 1987, Wines authored *De-architecture,* which summarized the firm's philosophy of Deconstruction as a union of sculpture and architecture. He was named chairman of the Department of Environmental Design at Parsons School of Design in 1986.

ACKNOWLEDGMENTS

Thank you to Paula Rice Jackson, who introduced me to my editor at Abrams, Lois Brown, who in turn deserves thanks for being such an enthusiastic and helpful support throughout the project. To my researchers, Gregory Littleton, text, and Dominique Lalli, photos, who pursued all leads with constant energy and willingness, I am very grateful. To Samuel Antupit, my appreciation for participating in this book from the very beginning and for bringing his special design talent to its visual presentation.

PHOTOGRAPHY CREDITS

Page 1: Thomas J. McCavera; Pages 4-5: Alan Karchmer; Pages 6-7: George Hein; Page 8: Peter Aaron/Esto; Page 9: Jerry Cappel; Pages 10-11: courtesy Vignelli Associates; Pages 12-13: Langdon Clay; Page 14: Carl Fischer; Page 16: Richard Payne; Pages 20-21: courtesy Skidmore, Owings & Merrill; Page 22: AP/Wide World Photos; Page 23: Robert Damaro, courtesy The Museum of Modern Art, New York; Page 24 (bottom): AP/Wide World Photos; Page 25: courtesy Venturi, Rauch and Scott Brown; (center left): Tom Bernard; (center right): Matt Wargo; (bottom): Paul Warchol; Page 26: Ezra Stoller/Esto; Page 27: Stephen Tucker; Page 28 (top): Peter Aaron/Esto; (center): Horst Thanhauser; (bottom): Peter Aaron/Esto; Page 29: Paschall/Taylor; Pages 30-31: Alan Karchmer; Page 31 (center left and right): Norman McGrath; Page 31 (top): Stanley Tigerman; Page 32: Paschall/Taylor; Page 33: William Taylor; Page 34: The Walt Disney Company; Page 35 (top): Peter Maus/Esto; (bottom): The Bettmann Archive; Page 36: Richard Payne; Page 37: Wolfgang Hoyt; Page 38 (top and center): Jaime Ardiles-Arce; (bottom): George Cott/Chroma Inc.; Pages 40-41: Paul Warchol; Pages 42-43: George Hein; Page 44: Photofest; Page 45: Aldo Ballo, courtesy Artimide; Page 46: Norman McGrath; Pages 46-47: courtesy Holly Solomon Gallery; Page 48: Robert Perron; Page 49 (top): Jon Naar; (bottom): Ballo & Ballo; Page 51: Murphy/Jahn; Page 53 (top): Langdon Clay; (bottom): Michael Datoli; Page 54 (top): Paul Warchol; (bottom): courtesy Knoll International; Page 55: courtesy Krueger International; Page 56: Peter Aaron/Esto; Page 57 (top): AP/Wide World Photos; (center): courtesy Panasonic; (bottom): courtesy Southwestern Bell Corporation; Page 59: courtesy NASA/Future Systems; Page 60 (top): Bernd Billmayer; (bottom): courtesy Michael McCoy; Page 61 (bottom): Tom Yee; Page 62 (top and center): Tom Wedell; (bottom): Abbey Sadin; Pages 64-65: courtesy SITE; Page 66: Photofest; Pages 68-69: courtesy SITE; Page 70 (top): Harry Shunk; (bottom): Jon Naar; Page 72: Tim Street-Porter; Page 73: Michael Moran; Page 76 (top left): Tim Street-Porter; (top right): Tom Bonner; (center): Tim Street-Porter/Esto; (bottom): Tim Street-Porter; Page 77 (top): Tim Street-Porter/Esto; (bottom): Tom Bonner; Page 78: Gordon Matta-Clark; Page 80: Norman McGrath; Page 81: Stanley Tigerman; Page 83 (top): Langdon Clay; (bottom): Samuel DeSanto/Esto; Pages 84-85: Sal Lopes; Page 86 (top left): Michael Kanouff; (top right): Christopher Irion; (bottom): Max Protetch and Elias Moser; Page 88 (top): Andreas Sterzing; (bottom): Peter Paige; Page 89: Durston Saylor; Pages 92-93: Alex Naar; Page 94: Iain Macmillan; Pages 96-97: Ivan Pintar; Page 98 (top): NYTimes Pictures; (bottom): George Hein; Page 100 (left): George Hein; (right): Jaime Ardiles-Arce; Page 101: Jonathan Hillyer; Page 103 (top): Peter Meyer; (bottom): Paul L. Wertheimer; Pages 104-5: Morley Baer; Page 106: Jon Naar; Page 107: courtesy WOET-TV, Dayton; Page 108 (top and center): courtesy WOET-TV, Dayton; (bottom): Brenda Huffman; Page 109 (center): Tom Lohman of Christian Studios Inc.; (bottom): Chad Floyd; Page 112 (top): Rex McManamy; (center): Jon Naar; (bottom): Steve Rosenthal; Page 113: Norman McGrath; Page 115: Jon Naar; Page 117 (top): Jon Naar; (bottom): Robert Harris; Page 118 (top left): Steve Rosenthal; (top right): Wolfgang Hoyt; (center): Murphy/Jahn; (bottom): AP/Wide World Photos; Page 119: NYTimes Pictures; Pages 120-21: Jon Naar; Page 122: courtesy Mitchell/Marza Architects, Hanover, New Hampshire.

INDEX

Numbers in italics refer to the illustrations